How Not to Be a D**k

The Subtle Art of Caring a Little Bit More Than You Did Before

By

Gary O'Toole

For Clare, my wife and
my children
Holly and Matilda.

INTRODUCTION

Once upon a time…

Congratulations, you are a dick! Now hold on, let me explain. You've picked up and started reading a book called How Not To Be A Dick, which means, in general terms, on some level, some deep rooted and untapped level, you recognise in yourself a degree of dickishness and that my friend, right there, that's a good thing, now we can begin to change and grow and be better people, good shit like that, unless you stole this book from the library (assuming they still exist) in which case, you really are a dick! But congratulations to me because my mother fucking book made it into a God damned library!

I digress.

So, what is this book about? Well, first of all, I have to come straight up clean, I am a dick, I'm not quite as dickish as I once was, and I'm working on being less dickish every day, but like most human beings, I'm a work in progress and guess what, you are too! I've had a few situations recently, where friends have needed some advice or input, or just a different perspective on an issue or problem they have had, I've offered my support, advice and my take on their situations and pretty much all of them liked what I was saying and how I was saying it. A couple suggested I recorded some of these little nuggets of wisdom and here we are.

Now you may be sat there thinking what qualifications does this guy have to dole out advice? Easy, I have none, I don't have a degree in anti-dick or anything like that, but I do have, at the time of writing, fifty-five years of life experiences. That's right people, I'm playing the life card! That's a big ass card to play so early in the game, but I did it!

Experience in both being a dick and in trying to not be a dick. Sometimes I have succeeded and sometimes I have spectacularly failed. I hope you get to learn from both as you navigate this book.

Okay, wait a minute, I want you to be a confident, proactive and respectable leader who are considerate, encouraging AND humble! Are you kidding me! Who am I talking to The Dalai Lama? I get it, I do. It's a lot to take in, a lot to digest, process and work through. Ultimately, if everything goes according to plan, there'll be 52 'lessons' in this book. That's one a week for a year.

A day to read and mentally consolidate, and six days to put practice into reality.

Besides, some of these things, unless you're a complete sociopath, you're probably the living embodiment of anyway, some... You might need to work on a little bit (Smiley face emoji).

I have self appointed myself the Henry Higgins of anti-Dickishness. I'm going to cover some random subjects, pick the ones you like and stick with them, discard the ones you don't like and put a pin in the ones you think you'd like to implement and get back to them later. Most subjects will cover a broad(ish) topic. I can't write a chapter on every single possible outcome for every possible situation, but I'll try and hit enough notes that the tune makes sense, I'll work on that metaphor.

Ready? Good, let's get into this.

Table of Contents

BE THE NOW 1
LIAR, LIAR, PANTS ON FIRE 3
THAT MEANS YOU, DUMB ASS 5
DO BETTER 7
SMILE, YOU CHEESY SCHMUCK 10
JUST SHUT UP AND LISTEN 13
BE A YES-ER, NOT A NO-ER 16
PUT A YOU AFTER A THANK 18
INNER PEACE 21
NOT RADIOACTIVE 24
FOLLOW THE LEADER 26
R.E.S.P.E.C.T, WHAT DOES IT MEAN TO YOU? 28
MANNERS MAKETH EVERYONE 32
DON'T FORGET THE CORNERS 34
REMAIN FAITHFUL, IF YOU CAN 36
ANYONE SEEN MY PEN 38
STEP ASIDE, I'VE GOT THIS 41
I'M GONNA DO THAT FOR SURE 44
COME ON KID, YOU CAN DO IT 46
HUMILITY IS HUMBLING. 48
TWO SUGARS PLEASE 50
REMAIN OR BECOME OPEN MINDED 53
YES! THEY SAID NO 57
BACK OF THE NET 59
I'M GONNA PASS 62
DON'T B FLAT PLEASE 65

I DON'T WANT TO PUT IT IN THERE	68
I AIN'T DOIN' IT FOR YOU BABY	70
I AM FUCKING EPIC	73
A DREAM IS WHERE A HOPE LIVES	76
IT'S GOOD TO LET ONE GO	78
MAIN PLAYERS TO SET	82
IT'S ALL YOU NEED	87
BE GOOFY	91
YOU CAN RING MY BELL	95
WHO DOESN'T LIKE A PAGE TURNER?	97
NIGHT, NIGHT, SLEEP TIGHT	99
AND A ONE, AND A TWO…	105
H TWO OH, I SEE	108
ANYONE GOT A LIFE JACKET?	111
PEACE OFF	115
YOU BE DOCTOR, I'LL BE NURSE	120
SPACE, THE FINAL LUXURY	123
THROW THAT SHIT OUT	125
HOW TO AVOID THE C-SPOT	129
WANNA GO PLAY?	134
SO, THIS IS A YES DAY	140
I'M OBJECTIONABLE	143
I'M NOT WRONG, YOU'RE WRONG, SHUT UP!	146
AIN'T NO KID GONNA SAY YES TO THIS BS	149
WHAT IS MY WHY?	153
HOW TO GET TO CARNEGIE HALL	155
Conclusion.	157

BE THE NOW

adjective
being, existing, or occurring at this time or now; current

I have two kids, one of whom is a teenager and it would be easier sometimes to pry candy from a diabetic toddlers sweaty clenched fist than remove my daughters phone from her hand. She lives, eats, breaths, sleeps, walks and talks with this thing. It is a constant, like the Northern Star or the need for oxygen, but when we DO manage to remove it from her, she connects, she engages, she joins in and she's fun. She's actually quite a smart cookie and has some interesting things to say if she's prepared to talk and I'm prepared to listen and the easiest way to do that is to lose the technology. It's a little bit ironic, don't you think (thank you Alanis Morissette) that as phones get smarter, we appear to be getting dumber.

Everything is quick, instant access and easy to control. If I could go back in time and Un-invent something, I think it would be the smart phone. Don't get me wrong, I have one, it's like a mini mobile office and I get a lot done on that phone and it's awesome, but like jokes at a funeral, there has to be a time and a place. So set boundaries for them and stick to it. Set a time when technology has to be put away and for the sweet love of baby Jesus Stick to it! You falter, fail or weaken, just once, and that weakness will be exploited into every argument you will ever have again with your kids about said technology, BUT here's the rub, you have to do the same. Once they've gone to bed, you can scroll your ass off until two in the morning (But don't do that) just don't let your kids bust you, you're screwed if they do. We also have a policy of no technology at the meal table. Notice I said meal, not dinner. I'd argue this policy be set in place for all meals, breakfast, lunch and dinner, it's a great habit to develop and lock in and once my kids realised there was no wriggle room on this one, they got on board and there's never any fuss.

It's okay to miss the latest Tweet or Snapchat message or Instagram post. It's okay to not know what Geoff had for his dinner or why Sandra don't like bees, it's all nonsense anyway and the sooner we realise that, the better. You can live without technology for the thirty minutes it'll take the kids to begrudgingly eat the meal that they're not going to appreciate anyway, but they will appreciate the connection, the conversation and the real human interaction. They might not understand, appreciate or realise this right away, but stick with it, they will.

This goes for the parents, partners, friends, co-workers and strangers too. Being able to talk to someone IS a skill, in fact it's a really difficult skill to master. Even now I know people who genuinely struggle to either start or maintain a conversation. For them, words and connections are difficult. It goes against the natural grain of their personality and takes real effort, but like all skills, they require practice and just like all skills, they can be learned. If you're a single guy eating a TV dinner alone in your underpants reading this, you get a free pass, but this skill goes way beyond removing technology at meal times. If someone has taken the effort to talk to you, it's not unreasonable for them to expect you to take a similar level of effort to listen to them and visa versa. Engage, be present. We can all be a little more focused, a little more present, a little more understanding, that's how conversations work. It's an unwritten contract and no smart phone or tablet is required.

LIAR, LIAR, PANTS ON FIRE

We all lie
Liar.
Noun
A person who lies.

It's true we do lie. I know I do, for the first ten years of their lives I told my kids about Santa Clause, the Tooth Fairy and all manner of stuff like that. Does that make me a bad parent or a bad person, of course it doesn't, I'm not talking about that kind of lie, I'm talking about the other kind, the kind that hurts, stings, and sometimes can't be taken back or forgiven. There are two lies, only two and these are them, the ones you tell yourself and the ones you tell others. This might even be the same lie. The ability to be truthful and honest with oneself is vital for development and growth, besides lying takes effort and a brilliant memory and I've got neither, so for me it was easy, I just chose to be honest. Now I've taken it to the extreme, I'm brutally honest. I'm not hurtful in my honesty.

In fact I try and be diplomatic in my honesty and specifically not hurtful, but if my wife, for example, asks if I think something she's wearing is nice or not and I don't like it, I tell her I don't like it and why and now, instead of being upset with my opinion, she welcomes it, because she knows its coming from a truthful place, not a hurtful place and she'll either wear it or not, depending on what she ultimately wants to do, her call, just as it should be.

Taste, after all, is subjective and it doesn't really matter if I like something she wears, it matters that she does. She might like it more IF I like it too, but she must have liked the item herself anyway, in order for her to buy it. I wear outlandishly bright socks, my wife thinks I'm weird, but I still wear them because I like them AND it stops the rest of the family wearing my socks all the time, because they can't find their own. They would much rather go look for their own socks, that wear mine-win.

Honesty does other things too. I'd argue a honest person probably sleeps better than a liar, they are probably happier too and because you're seen as a honest person, you're probably perceived, rightfully, as someone who's more trust worthy and reliable. Now, irrespective of your gender, you need balls to be honest, or more accurately, it takes courage to have the courage of your convictions and say what you mean and mean what you say. That's the external lie, the lie to others, but how do you deal with the lie you tell yourself? It might be a little lie.

"One more biscuit won't hurt, I'll start my diet tomorrow'

"I'm happy in this relationship/job/body"

It might be you're not purposefully hiding information from yourself, more that you might just be blocking things out on a subconscious level, you MIGHT not even know you're lying to yourself, but then again, you might know, deep down, exactly what you're doing, or not doing. How you identify with yourself, your sexuality, how you feel about a family member, your partner, your job. It could be one lie, it could be several, either way, at some point the house of cards you've built up around yourself will coming crashing down and you need to know how to deal with that shit before it happens. I could, and many people have, go on about the works of Nietzsche, Jung, Fraud, Kierkegaard and others, but that's some heavy duty stuff right there, like therapy kind of material and this book ain't that, but let's touch on therapy, just for a moment. Many, many, many people have found closure on issues they have had through therapy and it may very well be something that you need to consider, even if it's to dismiss it, but talking to a professional, outside your circle or inner circle can be very liberating and cathartic. After all, if you, I don't know, if you don't love your partner any more, its going to be difficult to discuss that with your actual partner. I'd argue it's a conversation that you are ultimately going to have to have, for your sake and theirs, but a therapist might help you organise your thoughts, so they are easier to process and work through. Nowadays finding a therapist is downright simple, there are apps that can help you find one, heck, you can even Google who's closest to you. I can't stress enough how vital it is that, if you feel you need help, for the love of God, your safety and the sanity of your friends and family, seek help. There are organisations, support groups, councillors and therapists, but like I said, this is not a therapy book, but perhaps also, one of the best ways to make sure you're not a dick, is to get yourself 'right' mentally. You'll also have to cover off emotionally, physically and, in one form or another, spiritually. More on these crazy ass topics in the pages to follow

.

THAT MEANS YOU, DUMB ASS

COMPASSION Has an ass in the middle of it
The dictionary definition of compassion is:
Feeling or showing sympathy and concern for others.

The definition of Sympathy, should you ask, is:

Feelings of pity and sorrow for someone else's misfortune.

Sympathy, concern, pity and sorrow, these are all incredibly strong words that evoke equally strong emotions and whilst these words can be looked upon as dark or negative words, the response they (hopefully) elicit should be light and hopeful.

"I sent Geoff home today on compassionate leave"

"I feel so sorry for Sandra, I can't imagine what she's gone through"

But what if we went a little further?

"I sent Geoff home today on compassionate leave, I'll give him a call later, make sure he's okay"

"I feel so sorry for Sandra, I can't imagine what she's gone through, I might take a bottle of wine round to her place tonight, have a chat about everything".

But what if we went a little further?

"I'll drive you home Geoff, make you a cuppa tea. You can talk if you want to, I'm here if you need me"

"Come on Sandra, I'm coming round and taking you out for lunch, we can have a good old catch up about everything, I'm here if you need me"

Every time I go into Melbourne I purposefully buy a homeless person a cup of coffee and something to eat. I tell you this, not to say hey, look at me, look how awesome I am, because I'm not-it's just a coffee and it's just a pie or a chocolate bar or something, it makes almost no difference, but imagine if we all did it? Imagine if we just took five minutes to buy some poor soul a coffee and had a quick chat with them? Australia has a very small number of people living in it, around 27 million people at the last count. There should be NO homeless people, there should be NO poverty, there should be no need for charities that help cloth, feed and educate our nations children, but there is. Cheap, affordable housing is an option, reeducation is an option, medical treatment for mental illness and depression, as prime examples, is available. We as a society could be doing so much more, even if that so much more is 'just' holding our politicians accountable and answerable and/or buying just one person a coffee and a chocolate bar.

That's BIG compassion though and quite frankly, we don't only have to focus on the big compassion, we can focus on the small compassion too.

Your friend broke a nail.
Your friend missed their bus.
Your kid is upset because they broke up with their partner.

It does not matter, it could be one of a million things, what matters is your mindset and response going into these situations and your mindset coming out the other side. If you've made the conscious decision to at least try and be more compassionate, then you will succeed. You'll succeed because you're trying and if you fail six times out of ten, then you got it right 40% of the time, which is still pretty awesome! Then try for 45%, then 50%. Pretty soon, you know what you'll be? A compassionate person and everyone looks at a compassionate person with awe and wonder.

"How did they become SO compassionate?"

I'll tell you how, they practiced. They listened and learned and got involved in the human race. Not just the human race that we think might help us, but the human race that we might be able to help without asking for anything whatsoever in return, well perhaps a little slice of pay it forward.

DO BETTER

Show kindness to yourself, and others
Kindness
noun
The state or quality of being kind

So, what is being kind, or showing kindness? It's not compassion, but being compassionate is, it could easily be argued, an extension of kindness. Yet kindness is so much more than compassion. If you send someone a birthday card for example, that's a kindness, but you're not showing sympathy, concern or pity, the traits of compassion. You're showing a willingness to participate in that person's celebrations. That involvement might only stretch to the card, you might not meet, see or communicate with them in any other way, think birthday card for Uncle Dave who lives half way around the world, in another time zone. You might not be able to physically celebrate with him, but he knows you are thinking of him, that brings him joy and you've just shown an act of kindness (and love) that will ultimately remind your Uncle that he is loved. Kindness is a word, smile, touch. Kindness is getting a grocery product off a high shelf for a little, old person shopping. I use this example because we all know that old people are all four foot tall and have very short arms! It's making your partner a cup of tea/coffee, or pouring them a glass of wine, when they come home from and exhausting day at work.

When I was twenty-two years old, I started back packing through Europe. I'd eventually continue my travels around the world for just over three years. At the start of that journey I ended up being one English pound short of my coach fare to travel from inner London to the international airport, I'd just miscalculated the English money I'd need because I'd never even considered the coach trip would cost FIVE quid! (robbing bastards)! But it didn't matter, they wanted five pounds, I had four! A little old lady (four foot tall with short arms) who I'd had a nice chat to at the station whilst we both waited for the same coach, she was NOT back packing, but still going to Europe, stepped forward and handed the driver a shinny gold one pound coin. To her, I'm sure, it wasn't much, but to me it was a beautiful act of kindness. She didn't want it back, she didn't want any fuss, she just saw someone who needed help and there she was, right at my side with a smile.

I served, for a while, in the British Army Reserves. In 2004 I was deployed to Basrah in Southern Iraq, where I would stay for the next eight months or so. If our base was being attacked with Mortars, and this happened more often than I'd like to remember, the incoming mail plane, that arrived every few days, couldn't land. This happened for well over a week. Ten days in the Iraqi dessert without the comforting words of loved ones is a VERY long time and we were going nuts, perhaps even a little stir crazy. Our communications with back home was what helped to ground us and remind us why we were doing the things we did. Eventually the plane did manage to land and our camp went into pandemonium. The line into the postal room extended right around the camp and everyone waited patiently in line to receive overdue communications from their loved ones. The air was electric and there was an almost festival feel to the waiting line, with everyone in very high spirits, laughing and joking and getting very excited at the prospect of what awaited them. I was no different, I waited for I think about three hours in that line to collect my mail, but when I finally got to the counter and offered my name, there was no mail. Nothing, not one letter. To say I was devastated would be to understate devastation. I crumbled into dust on the inside and I was crestfallen. I slowly walked across the parade ground, heading back to my accommodation. Half way across the parade ground I stopped, sucked in a huge lung full of oxygen and slowly sighed out. At just about the same time, a Staff Sergeant was walking across from the other side, presumably to collect her mail. She stopped, hung a left and headed for me. She stopped in front of me, extended her arms and gave me a much needed hug. It was warm and friendly and inviting and supportive. She released her grip, took a half step back and looked me dead in the eye.
"Sometimes we all need a hug" She said.
She smiled and walked off. I didn't know her. I didn't know her unit or where she was from, but she saw in me someone who desperately needed to connect to someone at that moment and she stepped in. I never saw her again, but again, I think of her often. She extended to me an act of kindness that has stayed with me for almost twenty years and she still makes me smile.

When I was seventeen, or so, I ended up renting a room in a house from two silver haired gentlemen who were, obviously, a couple. I had the attic room with a single bed, small fridge, single hob electric cooker and a tiny black and white television. I stacked shelves in the evening whilst I was going through college and I barely had enough money for food and rent, shit I could only afford clothes because everything I owned came from charity shops. About once a week I'd get a knock on my door, I'd open it and there would be the men, (I'll call them Stan and Dave). Stan always stood out front. He'd look back at a sheepish Dave.

"Hello love, listen, Dave's only gone and bought too much bloody shopping again, stupid sod! Anyway, we can't possibly eat all this, you couldn't be a love and take it off our hands could you? Honestly Dave, I could swing for you sometimes".
"Sorry Stan"
Smile.

I'd take the food, thank them and although I didn't have much, I'd offer them a couple of quid as a payment. They'd always smile and tell me not to be silly, I was doing them a favour. There would be a carton of milk, a tin or two of soup, a small box of teabags and a small loaf. Almost every week these guys did this, never asked me to 'do' anything weird or anything, they just saw someone who was struggling, but trying to better themselves, and decided they wanted to do something to help. Again, I think of those guys very often and I'm in awe of their generosity of spirit. Their kindness was profound and I'm left breathless by their actions. I have a deep love and respect for those two guys, and I wish they were still around, so I could tell them just how much of an affect they had on my life.

Kindness doesn't cost a thing. It doesn't cost financially or physically, but it pays dividends spiritually and emotionally. It only comes with a small risk, associated with 'opening' yourself up, becoming vulnerable, but the payout for kindness is immeasurable. People WILL remember you, and they'll remember you often and fondly and sometimes all it takes is a pound, or a kind word, or a small packet of homebred teabags. Try it out.

SMILE, YOU CHEESY SCHMUCK

verb

verb: smile; 3rd person present: smiles; past tense: smiled; past participle: smiled; gerund or present participle: smiling
Form one's features into a pleased, kind, or amused expression, typically with the corners of the mouth turned up and the front teeth exposed.

Look, I get it. Sometimes, especially over the last couple of years, it's tough to find a reason or two to smile, but hey, I'm here to help.
It takes eleven muscles in the human face and it takes a whopping forty-three to smile, so even if you don't want to smile, smile anyway, it's like a mini workout for your face and your face will thank you for it.
Have you ever been in a lift, for example, and someone starts to uncontrollably laugh? What happens? You laugh, the person next to you laughs and on it goes. Laughter is infectious and, to a degree, so is smiling. The trick isn't smiling, we can all smile, unless we have had a stroke or we have Bells Palsy or something, the trick is finding a reason to smile in the first place.

Some people have a natural smiley face, some like me, have resting bitch face. I'm not grumpy or sad or anything, it's just my face is, generally, set to neutral. I wish I had a naturally smiling face, but I don't. What I do have, is an ability to find a reason to smile in most situations…. Most.

I'm going to share a text conversation I had with a friend that was the actual reason for me writing this book. There are no identifiers, but I'll call my friend, for the purposes of this story Jane.

I've paraphrased slightly.

Me: "Hey Jane, How's things going?"

Jane: " Not too good, I started a second job for the same company I already work for today, absolutely hated every minute of it, then my boss came in to say hi and see how I was going and I was like Oh my God I hate it. She then told me she's likely going to sack a woman we've had working with us for ages, but who's a bit rubbish, and my boss said I'd get her shifts, if I liked. So it's safe to say this new job can sod off, I literally cried all the way home without trying that's how bad it was".

Me: "No, no, no! It was GOOD because your boss saw you hated the other job and told you more work, at the place I assume you like, would soon be coming up. If you didn't hate that second job, you wouldn't have had that conversation with your boss and there you go, karma patting you on the back, not kicking you in your ass!

Jane: " I LOVE your perspective! Thank you. Lightbulb moment! Can you please write another book about different perspectives?".

I said no, then I thought about it and changed my mind, and here we are.

My friend 'Jane' started the day crying and finished it smiling and she managed to do that because she had something to smile about, and that's the trick of smiling, and I mean *really* smiling, not that smile for the camera kind of smile, but the true, honest and open smile when you're using all of those forty-three muscles. You need to find something to smile about.

When my father died, I was heartbroken obviously, but I thought I was dealing with it pretty well, then after the funeral, several days later, as I was walking to work, I turned a corner and in front of me was the most beautiful Cherry Blossom tree I think I'd ever seen. Rich pink and white flowers hung from every millimetre of that tree, the air was thick with its heady fragrance and it was spectacular and… I burst into tears, right there, in the middle of the street, like some demented idiot. I could not pull my shit together, in fact my shit was flinging off and hitting as many metaphorical fans as it could, and this wasn't movie crying, it was ugly crying, you know the kind with red eyes and snot! I was overwhelmed with the realisation that this beauty was something my Dad would never see again, he's never see a Cherry Blossom tree blossom into anything as wonderful as what was in front of me right there and then. Then it hit me, of course he would, he was with me. You see, I'm Roman Catholic and for me, faith is important and I knew he'd see whatever he could, whenever he wanted. Now if you don't have a faith, that's obviously going to be difficult for you to get your head around and it won't work for you, but for me, it did and now, every time I see an Apple Blossom tree, I smile the broadest smile and instantly think of my father, it's truly magical and, almost twenty years later, it's never failed to make me smile. That's mine of course, you have to find yours. It could be a kid, a parent, putting on your favourite pair of socks (everyone else has favourite socks right, it's not just me)? It could be a piece of music, a text to or from an old friend, or someone you haven't connected with in a while.

It's strange, but smiling, while changing your external appearance will alter you internally. You smile on the outside, you'll smile on the inside too, I guarantee it and remember, face yoga, you heard it here first.

JUST SHUT UP AND LISTEN

Phrasal Verb
Shut up
Stop Talking.
Listen
verb
verb: listen; 3rd person present: listens; past tense: listened; past participle: listened; gerund or present participle: listening
Give one's attention to a sound.

There's an old saying in acting that a good actor acts, a great actor listens. Just take a moment to consider that, it's beautiful and so true. I always talk, my mind is often going at a thousand miles an hour in a hundred different directions. I talk to express ideas, tell jokes, fill the silence, because silent always needs filling (NB. It doesn't), but if you're having a conversation, easily the best thing you can do is truly listen to the other person. In some psychological fields it's suggested that, in an argument, people raise their voice because (subconsciously) they don't believe they are being heard. One of the best conversational tools I ever learned was this: parrot back. Let me provide you with an example.

Jane
"I don't believe in w because of x, y and z"
Me
"So what you're saying is because of x, y and z, you don't believe w?".
Jane
"Yes, that's exactly what I mean".

The discussion can flow from there, in a million different directions, you can agree, disagree, agree in part, but offer an alternative solution, but, and this is the really important part, because Jane knows I've listened and heard her and understood her and I know she's listened and heard and understood me, there is a 99.9% chance this conversation will remain a conversation and not develop into a full blown argument. You CAN disagree with someone, and them you, without it turning into a bloody battle, just watch a debating team, they're not raising their voices or slagging each other off, because they have taken themselves out of the equation and are listening to their opponent. Life should be a debating team and in many ways it is. We debate all the time, most of the time not even knowing we are doing it.

Be strong and confident in your choices and what you want to say, but be prepared to listen and, if need be, change your point of view. If you're having a discussion with someone and they genuinely change your mind on a subject, it could be anything, but if they have truly made you think, reconsider and ultimately change your mind about something, embrace that shit. Own it, it's yours.

"You know Jane, I thought you was talking out of your ass, but turns out I actually like most of what you're saying and I'm man/woman/person enough to accept that you've changed my mind"

Can you imagine how many arguments, conflicts and wars would be stopped before they have even started if we could manage that? But truth is, we can't always change our minds, or change someone else's. Some principles and thought processes are hard wired into us and we are never gonna change those, not for no one, not no how. In that case, what do you do with those people?

Take them into a field and shoot them!
No, we don't do that, that was just a joke, please don't shoot anyone!

You say something along the lines of:

"I've listened to what you've said and whilst you make some very strong point, I'm gonna have to stick with my original feeling about W. I understand where you're coming from and I've enjoyed discussing it with you, but for right now, we're sticking with w"

If it's a co-worker type thing, either you will sort it out, or your manager will. If you're the boss, you set the agenda, If you're the worker listening to their boss, do what you are told (Within reason and the guide lines surrounding your position, every job has one) and if your boss is asking you to do something you are uncomfortable with or does not fall within your job description, don't do it. They can shout, argue, shake their fists, bang on car does and threaten to sack you, but don't you dare do something outside your scope of practice or job description OR it makes you feel uncomfortable.

If your partner says
"We have no money left in this weeks budget and we've only got a cauliflower and some cheese in the fridge, what do you want to do about dinner?".
And you shout
"I want a steak!".
Then you are an idiot and deserve grey slop for dinner six nights a week. What your partner just said was:
"We are broke, there's no money left and we really need to use what we have in the fridge, because we can't afford to buy anything else, please say you'll have cauliflower cheese for dinner, I'll make it delicious"

They spoke, you didn't listen, again, you're an idiot.

BE A YES-ER, NOT A NO-ER

Remain or become optimistic
adjective
adjective: optimistic
Hopeful and confident about the future

I've said remain optimistic, but truthfully, you might not be able to remain optimistic, especially if you wasn't optimistic to begin with. So perhaps I should start, more accurately with, become optimistic.

Something that I say every time I'm asked the question "Are you a glass half full, or a glass half empty kind of guy?" I say exactly the same thing, every single time:

"My glass is 100% full. Half with water and half with Oxygen"

It's a little twee, probably a bit annoying, but I do genuinely believe it, I don't know how to be anything else but optimistic. Am I confident about the future? No, not really, but I am hopeful. What's the alternative? Was I confident I'd finish writing this book, getting it to a publisher or selling a copy? No, but again, I was hopeful and perhaps hopeful is all we can wish for right now.

At the time of writing this, the world is in the second year of dealing with Covid19. Melbourne, where I live, is in its SIXTH lockdown, longest lockdown in global history! Fun fact for you there. Everyone is stressed and suffering, but I have to remain hopeful that we will find a way through this. The other side of this might not look exactly like what we had hoped it would, but there will be 'the other side' of this, at some point. I'm hopeful we'll mostly get vaccinated, or up to 80% and borders will re-open, travel is allowed, people can rebuild their lives and careers and businesses. I'm hopeful that the gyms will open again and I'll try and do something about the fact I put on so much Covid weight I can't see my feet when I look down, but I'm confident I'll fix it and I'm confident there'll be no more home fucking schooling, which infuriates my kids and makes me look stupid as shit. There's a very good reason I'm not a teacher!

BUT, what does that mean for me and, equally importantly, what does that mean for you? Am I suggesting you walk around like a dumb idiot, smiling at everything and "Always looking on the bright side of life"? No, it's not that I think that's a task that is impossible, but I do think it's a task most of us are not able to spend enough time on to achieve. Instead, focus on the little wins. A win after all bolsters optimism. If you're a boxer and you've lost your last seven fights, going into fight number eight, I'd argue you're not gonna be too fucking optimistic, but if you've won the last eight fights, I'm pretty sure you'll be confident you'll knock your opponent on their ass. It doesn't mean you will, of course, but an optimistic outlook will help you achieve more and go further than someone who hasn't got any, so practice optimism. You have to be present, you have to commit and believe and practice what you preach, even if that preaching is internal and despite everything life throws at us, individually and as a culture, there is always something to remain optimistic about. It's 'just' about flipping a negative thought on its head, no short order to be sure, but start with one thought, then try another, consolidate that with a third and on and on and on. Pretty soon, you'll be an optimist. Not a head in the clouds kind of optimist, but someone who can apply the principles of optimism to everyday life and squeeze the best out of everything they come in contact with. Try it, then try it again. I'm optimistic about your ability to succeed! (See what I did there!).

PUT A YOU AFTER A THANK

How to be or become grateful

adjective
adjective: grateful
Feeling or showing an appreciation for something done or received.

You know what shits me, what really shits me? Bad manners, there's just no need for them. Someone, way smarter than me, said manners cost nothing and whoever said it was right on the money, manners don't cost a single cent. Seems like the words please and thank you are becoming as rare as hens teeth, simply impossible to find. Now, this might be a generational thing, but… there's always more to it than that, you know that, I know that, we all know that. A typical statement from someone of my generation might be:

"Kids today have no manners. They don't know how to say please and they sure as hell don't know how to say thank you".

Well, that might be true, but that's not entirely their fault. It's OUR generation who should be teaching them. We have to tell our kids to say please, thank you, be respectful, show your manners. Sure some kids are failing themselves, but we are failing them too, especially if we are blaming them for not doing something we should have taught them in the first place. So before you bang on about "This bloody generation" remember who made 'em! Us!

With that in mind, lead by example. Now, you do have to contextualise the words too, don't just say them parrot fashion and not actually mean it, you'll end up sounding condescending, arrogant and/or shallow, not three great traits to have, if I'm being honest. So if the waitress/waiter comes up and offers to refill your coffee, say thank you and mean it. They will know, one way or another, and if you say thank you with confidence, commitment and a smile, you've just knocked that ball out of the damned park. They will remember you and you would have gone some way towards making their day a better day, and who doesn't want a better day?

Now, you could be out for a long walk in the sun and be grateful for some shade, you do not have to show the shade gratitude, that would be stupid and you would require psychological attention, again, as with everything, be considerate with your responses, by which I mean consider your responses. Tone here is everything, tone and intent. We've all had someone say "Thank you" in such a way that you know what they're really saying is "Go fuck yourself" (Or is that just me?) I don't think it is. Someone who really doesn't want to be where they are, doing the thing they are doing and somehow, subconsciously, blame you for forcing them to continue doing the thing they hate. They may not be grateful, but you still can be, you can rise above the tone and inference. If someone shows you to your seat "Thank you" someone comes over to serve you, "Another one of these please," they come back "Thank you". You WILL wear that person down and you will make a difference to their day. The thing is, everyone carries around baggage, every single one of us and you have no idea, unless you get into a deeper conversation with someone, what that baggage might be. That waitress might have been a real bitch, but she might be struggling to cover the rent, she might have gotten up late and missed breakfast, she might be in an abusive relationship, her grandfather might be in hospital dying, there is an infinite number of possibilities as to why someone is not nice to you, but again, their problems are not your problems, so take a deep breath, smile and say thank you.

That's showing gratitude, which is awesome, but we also need to cover off being grateful which can be different and more complex to achieve. For arguments sake I'm going to say showing gratitude is applying a principle to something externally, you're grateful the waitress brought you a fresh coffee, for example. I'd say being grateful is something you internalise. Now an internal can and should manifest itself as an external gratitude, but an internal gratitude could relate to pretty much everything. You've been ill and you are grateful for your health. You worked hard at Uni and you're grateful for the support of your teachers, after receiving some great grades. You're grateful for having a decent family who supported you or a girlfriend/boyfriend who did the same. You can literally be grateful and show gratitude towards absolutely anything and I am, for the most part, that person. I'm not entirely grateful to the arsehole who cut me up on the freeway, but then again, should I be? Should I be grateful because he/she made me more aware of my environment, watching other cars closer than I had before, or grateful that we didn't crash and highlight how better I am at driving than I thought? It's not the situation you're faced with, it's how you face that situation. Mindset is everything and as with all mindset things, they can be learned, practiced, developed and honed.

And tip your waitress, she needs those tips to survive!

INNER PEACE

noun
noun: serenity; noun: serenities
The state of being calm, peaceful, and untroubled.

Well, what does that mean and how the hell do you get there? I mean, how in the actual fuck do you become untroubled? We're all troubled in some way, shape or fashion, aren't we? I'm gonna say yes for you here, because I'm with you. Perhaps we should say a state of serenity is being calmer, more peaceful and less troubled? If you take a movie star-rich, famous, adored and respected, I guarantee they have insecurities: They're going to lose their fame, their money, their Hollywood status. That sounds pretty troubled to me, and if someone who we 'normal' folk considers someone who has everything they could possible want be troubled, what kind of chance do we have?

There's an old saying, "It's lonely at the top, but crowded at the bottom" So whilst the concept of someone who appears to have everything they need in life is troubled in some way is, for the most part, inconceivable to the rest of us, but being rich and famous isn't a cure all for anyone. Look at the divorce rate amongst celebrities, look at the suicide rates or the countless reports of depression. So, neither money, fame or adulation can bring on a calm, peaceful or serene mind, so we're levelling the playing field. On this one, we are all at ground zero. You're as likely to find peace of mind as a penniless pauper, as you are a rich and famous movie star, so how do we achieve these goals?

It may surprise you hear this, but one of the ways is, I believe, through meditation. I am blisteringly aware how New Age that sounds. I thought meditation was just for tree hugging hippies, but I downloaded a free app from my smart phone and gave it a crack and now I wouldn't be without it. Here's the reason why it works, it forces you to focus your mind. If you start thinking about something, anything, you take it back to focusing on just your breathing. We are bombarded, as a society, from the moment we wake up to the moment we go to bed. It's more than a little bit ironic that, it would appear, as phones get smarter, people are getting dumber. Everywhere you look, everyone is on a device, all the time (well for the most part). Everyone's got FOMO and it's all about the next like, follow or thumbs up and if society is constantly busy and we are constantly busy and our minds are constantly stimulated or flooded with information, meaningless or not, how the hell are we supposed to find serenity? If we don't do something to break that chain, then the answer is a simple one, we can't. We are stuck in this perpetual loop until the end of our meaningless, click bate filled, life.

So find that time, I implore you, I think it's vital. Put your phone down, close your laptop, switch off the TV and sit, still, in the silence. Close your eyes and concentrate on your breathing and just your breathing for five minutes-set a timer. When you're not doing anything, five minutes seems like a very long fucking time, an eternity, it takes forever! It feels like thirty minutes, easily. That shows you just how busy are lives and our minds have become and drowning in all that noise, you'll never find your serenity.

Take that five minutes however, building up to fifteen minutes if you can, and you will be amazed at what those few, brief, moments give you. You'll be more focused, more driven, more animated and alive. It's like you've plugged your brain in to a turbo charger. Your energy levels will spike and you'll become super productive.

What do you do if the noise isn't external, but internal? What if the thing blocking your ability to find serenity is you? You can lock yourself away from technology all you want, but you can't lock yourself away from yourself, you are literally everywhere you go! We tend to worry about one of three things, something that happened in the past, something that's happening to us presently or what will happen in the future.

The Past

We can and should all learn from the past, our past, but the thing to remember is, it's done. It's finished, it's over and there's nothing we can do about it except learn from it and move on. Think of it as an entry in a diary. You can read from it, see where you went wrong and hopefully, in the future pages you write, change the things you think need changing. The past is a prison you don't want to be trapped in, the past is a guide book, not a life sentence. Allow yourself to forgive, either yourself or someone else who you feel has wronged you and let that shit go. Holding on helps absolutely no one.

The Future

Likewise, the future is not written and you shouldn't allow yourself to be held hostage by it. You don't like the look of how something might go down, do something about it and change the outcome before it happens. Don't like where you live? Look for a different place. Don't want to be with your partner any more, leave them. Don't like the job you've got, or dream of another job altogether? Pursue your dream until it becomes a reality, then quit the job that sucks. If you're seventy-five and want to be an astronaut, then I'd say it's too late for you, unless you're a billionaire called Richard Branson, then you're good to go. For most people, you can do something about where your life is heading. Have a plan, build a road map and follow it.

The Present

This one, you've got. You absolutely can do something in the moment to be calm, relaxed and find serenity. Remove the noise and the distractions and just focus on yourself. After all, serenity doesn't come from external forces, it comes from within, so you have to look inward to find the answers. Take a moment to look for them and they will present themselves to you, you just have to be willing to find it and act upon it.

NOT RADIOACTIVE

adjective: proactive; adjective: pro-active
(Of a person or action) creating or controlling a situation rather than just responding to it after it has happened.

You've already been proactive. You picked up this book and started to read it. You are proactive a thousand times a day, but I'm not talking about those little, piss ant, proactivity wins, which in their own way are important. For example, I'm guessing everyone at work was pleased as punch that you were proactive enough this morning to put pants on! But I'm talking about bigger proactive actions, grand proactive actions that help change and define your lives. The kind of action that people write about in their autobiographies

So, how proactive do you have to be? Well, they say the average person takes ten years to become an over night success! Ha! You have to work your ass off day, noon and night to achieve your goal, assuming you have a goal to work towards in the first place? But what if you don't? Well, it's okay. It's okay to not have a plan, or to know what direction you're supposed to be going in, but that usually means you're treading water and if that's your thing, that's cool. There are many days, when I'm working eighteen hours a day when I wish I had a 'normal' life, stress and extra work free, but ultimately, for me, that's not how I operate. I like to be going full speed as long as I can do, seven days a week. I understand this isn't for everyone, but if it is for you, then you need a plan, a strategy, a short term and long term goal. In order to be proactive, you have to know where you're going, or at the very least, have a general idea of the direction you want to be going in, so first, set your self a mission statement, a single sentence that defines what you want to achieve and why you want to do it. If you haven't got your why, it's difficult to remain focused and you run the risk of failure.

I want an on line business so I can work for myself and be financially independent.

That's not a bad goal right? Work from home, be your own boss, be financially secure, great, but what do you do next?

Think about what you want to sell, where you'll source your product from, who's your market, how do you reach that market, how do you brand and package your product, how do you distribute your product and on and on it goes. You can't answer a single one of those questions if you're not proactive, if you don't go out there and do the work and you can't be proactive if you don't know what direction you're going in, so planning is key.

Assess, Plan, Implement and Evaluate A.P.I.E.

You might fail on your first attempt, you might fail on your second and third and…. You get the idea-ten year over night success! You might crush it and hit a home run straight off the bat and boy, do I hope you do! A.P.I.E applies to any situation. You don't want your own business, you 'just' want that promotion going at work, what you gonna do about it? What are you bringing to the table? If you're putting yourself up for a promotion, you need to shine like a fucking star in the heavens my friend, go that extra mile, finish that report way before time and make sure it's flawless, come in early, go home late, have 20 minutes for your lunch instead of the hour. Polish, shine, polish, shine and…. Dazzle! I'm not suggesting you do this for the rest of your working life, you'll only last five years, it'll burn you out and you'll die from stress or a stroke! But if you put yourself out there, if you're waving your arms in the air like a mad man, shouting "look at me, look at me," when someone does look at you, you need to burn their retina's out.

Do AT LEAST one thing a day that can, potentially, get you closer to your goal, because if I can only guarantee one thing, it's this: If you're not doing it, someone else IS.

FOLLOW THE LEADER

Are you a leader or a follower?
noun: leader; plural noun: leaders
1.
The person who leads or commands a group, organisation, or country.
noun: follower; plural noun: followers
1.
A person who supports and admires a particular person or set of ideas.

You can be either, if you're middle management, you can be both. You can easily be a follower who wants to be a leader, or better still, a natural born leader who always thought they were a follower, until people started following you.

Have you ever been to a seminar or in a classroom and there's an 'activity' (I fucking hate those things!) And someone just kinda takes charge? That there is your leader, your Alpha. Have you ever been in one of those things and someone else TRIES to take charge? That's another Alpha, sit back and watch these people duke it out, one of them will rule supreme. Everyone else, everyone following the directions of the Alpha, they're your Beta, they are your followers. Some people LOVE being a beta, some love being an Alpha, some just step up because no one else will-Still Alpha's, even if they didn't know it.

In the forces, we say a team is as strong as its weakest link. So if we're going on a 40 kilometre walk, we make sure we give the best, most uplifting and awe inspiring talks to the person who's struggling to maintain. We put them at the front, let them know we are in their hands, they've got this, they can do it, we are ALL there for them! And it works, every single time, it works. Why? Because they know we believe in them and their ability to push through the discomfort and mental pain. We give them purpose and a goal and so much support. That person may never become a fully fledged Alpha, but they will always know they have it in them, if they ever want to step up and release it. Good leaders lead from the bottom up, managers lead from the top down. Don't be a manager! Your work force will not appreciate it and you won't get nearly as much out of them. Instead lead your workforce to bigger and better things, inspire people to talk and communicate and develop ideas. Let them know they, and their voice, is something of worth within the organisation. You might not like their idea, it might be impractical, or tried before and failed, but be open to at least listening to them and then give them a reason why their idea won't work, or why you can't try it, or don't. Tell them what they have thought of is new and exciting and innovative and you can't wait to try it and see how it develops and then give them the credit they deserve for thinking of it! You do that, they'll do it again and again, I promise.

Individual style comes into play here, but for the most part, just like the armed forces, leadership can be taught. There are thousands of leadership courses and if that's the way you want to go, fill your boots. You know when people say "Oh, they are a natural born leader" well chances are 'they' are not. It takes time to develop those skills. Some people learn these skills remarkably quickly and well, some take time to mature into them.

R.E.S.P.E.C.T, WHAT DOES IT MEAN TO YOU?

adjective
adjective: respectful
Feeling or showing deference and respect.

Respect! There are songs written about it, there are books written about it, there are movies and poetry that deal with it, but ultimately, what is it? What does it mean to you and do you always get it, give it, require it or earn it? You might want all the respect in the world, but do you deserve it? Weird thing about respect, you can have it, but not feel it. It's like at the end of a relationship, when one person still loves the other, but the feelings are not mutual, it doesn't matter what the other person says or does, if you ain't feeling it, you ain't feeling it, and there's usually nothing you can do about it.

The first part of the adjective for respect is feeling or showing, but how do you 'feel' respect? It's not an emotion, it's a thought process, or at the very least, it's a mixture of the two. You can intellectualise respect all you want, you can apply it to a principal, for example, but if you don't feel as though you have it from someone you want it from, you very quickly realise you have very little time for that person any more, even if what they are trying to say, or convey, is a valid and valuable point. So let's break this down even further, let's break it down to a bit of give and a bit of take.

Giving.
adjective: **giving**
Providing love or other emotional support; caring.

IS respect an act of love? Have you ever even considered that? If we met for a drink in a cafe and I asked you to define respect, would your mind initially jump to love? Mine wouldn't, well not up until now, but if you think about it, it actually makes a lot of sense because isn't love the ultimate sign of trust? And shouldn't respect flow on from that, because, at some level, love and respect go hand in hand?

There's an old saying that goes something like this: You can't learn to love others until you've mastered the art of being able to love yourself. To put it another way, how can you show respect for someone else, when you're unable to truly respect yourself? You might respect yourself just fine, and that would be awesome, but what do you do if you don't? What if you're not quite there yet?

Here's a little exercise for ya. Write down ten things you like about yourself, go on, I can wait. Ten, not nine or eight, a solid ten, I'll be right here until you finished….

Okay, you got ten? Did you? Did you really, or did you just skip right to the next line in the book? You did! Well, that's fucking cheating dude and I ain't having it, write those ten fucking things down already, I've got shit to do!

You do it now? Great! Finally, you slack ass! So you got your ten. Was the list easy to write? Did it take you a long time? Do you BELIEVE what you wrote to be true?

Here's the thing about lists like this, when you manifest something by, I don't know committing it to a list for example, It is no longer a 'internal' thing, it's real, you can touch it, you've turned it into a 'real' thing and as a real thing, your brain absorbs it in a different way to your internal monolog. The thing is, we forget how awesome we are, we rarely look inside to see what's right and what needs our attention, you write ten things down, those words take on a stronger meaning, not a different meaning, but a stronger one. YOU begin to believe those words just a little bit more than you did before you wrote them. Read that list every day for three months and guess what? You REALLY believe in them and they begin to externally shape the person you are, by internally changing or reaffirming what you already believed in yourself to begin with. I'll wait while you comprehend just how blown your mind was by this revelation……

You do a thousand things a day that demand your respect, give yourself the gift of self respect, you're allowed and IF you still don't believe you've earned your own respect because of what's one that list, change the fucking list! It's your list, they are your words, it's your future, you are the Captain of your own ship, give in to the possibility of respect and you will get it, you know:

Build it and they will come, kind of shit.

I tend to automatically give respect to people. It's only when they screw up I fuck 'em off. Disrespect me and I'll burn you like an old bridge no one uses any more. This is just one of my many character flaws, and I'm very much aware of it, more over, it's not one that I've actively tried to fix just yet. You disrespect me and I'll drop you like a hot stone. That's not to say you can't work your way back into my good book, but you'll have to work your ass off to prove why I should take you back. Is that the bast way to be? Hell no, do better than me, I'm an idiot! I've pulled people up on being disrespectful before and their initial response most of the time?
"Oh shit no, I didn't mean it like that...."
People are stupid, on the whole, and we can sometimes try and say one thing and end up sounding like we've just said something completely different. Best to avoid this type of friendship destroying lunacy. Best you just parrot back what you just heard…
"I'm sorry, just to clarify, did you just say……."
If the person says yes, that's exactly what I just said, then they are being disrespectful and you can kick 'em in the clacker (But don't really, you'll get arrested, and then I'd feel terrible. Not terrible enough to post bail or anything, but kind pretty bad). I hope they use the former example of a mistake and offer both their apology and an explanation. Truth is you can't make someone respect you and if they don't respect you, remove them from your life. I don't care who it is, it can be your own fucking mother for all I care, you deserve better than to have them in your life, and the best way to make sure this kind of thing doesn't happen to you in the future is to remain respectful yourself and pull those people up on their lack of respect. Provide caring, love or other emotional support, hell you can even disagree with someone and still show them respect whilst arguing your point, now that's a skill.

At the same time, let's talk about the take part of this give and take scenario. Up to now we've talked about self respect, externalising your internal respect and giving respect to others. We've also touched on what to do with those people you come in contact with who don't show you the respect you deserve, and you do deserve it, but what do you do when someone is respectful to you? How do you handle it? What do you do or say or act? You've heard of the acronym KISS right? Keep It Simple Stupid. Well, do that, after all, that's what we want right? If you've earned someone's respect, work at keeping it, be strong, be committed, remain true. Respect isn't contained in a measured vessel, you can't run out of it, so spread it around and watch it grow into something quite spectacular.

MANNERS MAKETH EVERYONE

Be a gentleman/lady/other.
noun
noun: gentleman; plural noun: gentlemen
1.
a chivalrous, courteous, or honourable man."he behaved throughout like a perfect gentleman"
A man of good social position, especially one of wealth and leisure.
a man of noble birth attached to a royal household."a Gentleman of the Bedchamber"
2.
a polite or formal way of referring to a man."opposite her an old gentleman sat reading"

First of all, let me clear up my pronouns and nouns. I know there are many pronouns and nouns: Him, Her, Them, Them and so on. I use the pronoun him/his and the term gentleman only because grammatically and textually it makes sense. If I used all the pronouns every time I tried to say something, the book would be almost unreadable. It's not out of a sign of disrespect. I know many people in the LGBTQIA+ community and they deserve our respect and understanding and acceptance, but I am unable to do them justice here, other than to acknowledge them as an equal and intricate part of our global community and as a cis man, and given that I'm writing this in the first person, it's just easier for me to do so and although I know the term ladies and gentlemen is gendered, I couldn't find an appropriate Non-gendered alternative to convey the same point. Hope that makes sense.

So, what, for me, is being a gentleman? For me, it's about behaviour. Now there are some women who refuse to let a man open a door for them and refuse to step through a door opening by a man because they consider such an act sexist, and I'd agree, but I don't just hold the door open for women, I hold the door open out of respect and for anyone who's coming through it. I don't care if you're tall, short, fat, thin, black, white or any shade in-between. I don't care if you're young, old, male, female or any and all aspects of the LGBTQIA+ community. I don't care if you're standing tall, have a limp or you're in a wheelchair, If I get to that door before you, I'm holding it open until you walk through it. If I only did that for pretty, young women, then I'd be a sleazy sexist and I'd have earned your vitriol, but that's just not the case and I'd ask that you don't automatically jump to that conclusion when someone opens a door for you. Sometimes is just someone holding a door open. If a woman gets to the door first and holds it open for me, I'll say "No, after you" If anyone gets to the door before me, I'd say exactly the same. If they insist, I walk through smile and say thank you. I don't curse in front of people I don't know, I stand when someone leaves the table, or walks back to it.

Am I more chivalrous towards women, yes probably if I'm being honest, but I'm a husband and father to two beautiful girls and I'm surrounded by women all the time, 80% of the people I work with are women, so I am in contact with females probably 90% of my waking life, but I try to be equally as gentlemanly in the company of men. I don't truly know what it means to be a gentleman, but for me, it's about respect and being polite, it's about my behaviour, it's about my language and staying true to the best version of myself as I can be.

DON'T FORGET THE CORNERS

There have been entire books written about the importance and significance about making your bed in the morning, but ultimately it's about performing and completing your first task of the day. Think about it, within the first few seconds of waking up, you've achieved your first goal! That shit is magnetic and invaluable. It set's you up for wanting to achieve your next task and the one after that. It's the snow flake you push down a hill that becomes a snow ball, then a bigger one and bigger and faster and it soon becomes this unstoppable juanaght.

It'll instantly make your room look tidier and clutter free and you will, despite yourself, have a great sense of pride in your achievements. You are also developing very good habits. Once you've made your bed so often it's almost a morning ritual, you'll find you'll crave that feeling more and more in all aspects of your daily life. Good habits will naturally flow on from the bed making exercise. All of a sudden, you're clearing the cups and plates from your desk, it's easier to pick the clothes up off your floor. You bring the cups and plates out of your room and instantly pack the dishwasher, while you're in the kitchen, you might as well clean the surfaces while you're waiting for the dishes to clean and on and on it goes.

Plus, it's a small doable thing. I know whaat it's like. Someone on Twitter or TikTok or Facebook, or whatever tells you, you can achieve unbelievable goals if you only do a couple of things, one of which is usually sign up to their product! And BOOM! You eagerly open your first email from them and they list off twenty things you have to do, most of which are unrealistic, in the first week of the program. "You too can loose 40 Kg in a WEEK if you calorie count to 600 Cals a day. Cut out carbohydrates, sugar, refined or processed foods, red meat, alcohol and dairy. Oh, and you have to be in the gym for 6 hours a day, 4 hours on cardio and 2 on resistance training" and you read that and thing Holy fuck! I want my damned money back! None of that is achievable and guess what, you're right, it's not achievable, you'd be lucky to just give up the sugar! You know what is achievable? Making your damned bed! Its instant Karma, instant gratification and it sets you up for the day. You've been out of bed like 15 seconds and BANG! You've already achieved your first goal. After that, the second one doesn't seem so daunting. Consistent, persistence and achievable, what more do you want out of life?

So make your damned bed!

It also hard wires your brain into processing a task in a different way. You make your bed every day for 12 weeks and you know what you've done? You have rewired your brain into accepting a new task as a habit. Think about that for a second; You are directly responsible for reprogramming the most complicated computer in the world into bypassing the thought process behind the task. You'll wake up and just make your bed. You won't think about it, you won't process it, you won't deliberate about it, you'll just get up and make your bed! Now imagine if you did that for another task and another and another? Imagine if you did that 4 or 5 or 6 times a day. How many new pathways would you form? How many new habits would you develop? And all that starts with just making your bed, it's quite remarkable, when you think about it. Plus you have a really nice and tidy bedroom for when you wanna bump uglies with someone! Winner-winner chicken dinner.

REMAIN FAITHFUL, IF YOU CAN

noun: faith
Complete trust or confidence in someone or something.
Strong belief in the doctrines of a religion, based on spiritual conviction rather than proof.

Now it's important here to distinguish between a faith, dream or wish. I'm not talking "I have faith I'll get a puppy dog for Christmas" here, that's a wish, not even a dream and definitely not faith. Faith is when Granddad falls over and needs a hip replacement and you have faith he pulls through the surgery okay, but again, as in most things in this book, you scratch a little deeper and guess what, you go a little deeper.

You can have external faith, of course you can, just think of Granddad and his hip and there are the religious connotations of course, but the kind of faith I'm talking about here is not religious based. You can have a faith, of course you can, and no one can tell you to believe or not believe in a faith, that's entirely up to you. I'm a Roman Catholic and I have a strong faith, but this faith is not that (directly), it's about faith, I suppose, in yourself! You need to internalise some of that magic. You need personal faith, as in faith in the person and that person has to be you. You have to believe in something bigger than yourself, otherwise, what is there to strive for? What is there to work towards?

You're trying to sell something, a book, theatre tickets, a song, on line tee shirts, whatever it is, it's yours, you own it and you control it. If you don't have faith in your own product, how do you expect anyone else to? You have to have faith, faith in your product and/or faith in yourself to see the course and achieve your goals.

According to statistics, only 20% of millionaires inherit their wealth, the other 80% earned all that cash on their own and of them, on average, a millionaire has been bankrupt 3.5 times. I don't quite understand how you can be half bankrupt, but that's averages for you. Now bankrupt doesn't mean broke, down to your last dollar, bankrupt means going to court and officially declaring yourself bankrupt, heavy shit, but you know what those millionaires had? Faith silly! Faith that everything will work out in the end.

They picked themselves up, disked themselves down, got back on the horse, all that metaphor shit you hear about. They did NOT give up. They had faith that they would achieve their goals and the ones who stood up, started again? They succeeded!

Don't get me wrong, there was a bucket load of sweat, blood and tears behind those successes too. Sleepless nights, strong coffee, grit and determination, but behind all that hard work, 20 hour days and phone calls overseas at 4 O'Clock in the morning was…. Faith! They believed they would overcome their trials. They believed they were destined for greater things and that faith helped them manifest those dreams. Have faith in what you're doing, truly believe it and others will believe it too. People buy into people, not products. Those people who invest in your product are not investing in your product, dumb ass, they are investing in you! And remember this, don't ever let anyone tell you your idea is dumb. You've had an idea, you're already smarter than most people in the room, run with that. If you do let the naysayers put you off, then you're as dumb as they are and you deserve not to succeed. Having said that, be defined by your wins, not your failures, and a win might just be not giving up after the tenth attempt. I think Thomas Edison designed the lightbulb over one hundred times before he got it right, suck on that defeatists!

ANYONE SEEN MY PEN

Start a journal

noun: journal; plural noun: journals
1. A daily record of news and events of a personal nature; a diary.

Why the hell would I do that? Haven't I got enough to do in a day already? Well, yes you do, but there are many benefits to keeping a journal, chief amongst them are these;

They provide an opportunity for positive self-talk and reenforcement of ideas. I, like millions I suspect, talk to myself, I talk to myself all the time. I do this primarily to consolidate a thought process. Saying something, or writing it down, makes it seem somehow more real. The benefit of writing something down, of course, is that you don't have to worry about forgetting it. The same can be said about negative thoughts, writing them down clearly identifies the issue and if you've identified something, you can fix it, change it or irradiate it.

Similarly, it helps you organise your thoughts, it's just like jotting down your mental 'to do' list. Knowing what you did today and what you have to achieve tomorrow sets you on a clearly defined path. If you read your journal right after making your bed, the world is yours my friend.

It's a great stress release. This is called a brain dump and I love a good dump! All the clatter and noise you have rattling around in your melon, making all that noise, dump it in your journal and it's actually been shown to reduce feelings of anxiety and stress.

People sometime ask me "What did you do over the weekend?" I tell them I can hardly remember what I had for breakfast, and it's true, sometimes I can't, but a journal helps improve your memory. One, you can actually reflect on what you've written and self reflect on your day and two, you've got to remember what it was you actually fucking did in the first place, in order to write it down.

As a writer, I have a thousand ideas a day. Sometimes a story idea, a line of dialogue, a tag line for a movie screenplay or something for another children's book. If I didn't write them down, 90% of those ideas would be totally and completely forgotten.

It helps to reduce intrusion and avoidance symptoms post trauma and is believed to be particularly helpful for people suffering from PTSD or a history of trauma. It helps the writer compose a coherent narrative, structuring their experiences and allowing them to process that information more effectively.

It can be quite useful to use the acronym W.R.I.T.E which stands for What topic, Review and reflect, Investigate, Time yourself, Exit smart.

Describe what happened, how it made you feel, investigate why it made you feel that way, write for at least five minutes a day, don't plan the words, let them flow and finally reread what you have written, reflect on it and figure out what you can gain from the experience. Try starting with something like "As I read my journal, I noticed that……"' or "I feel…." Both great lead in lines.

Whatever you decide to write or how you chose to journal, there are thousands of papers on the benefits of doing so. I keep mine under lock and key. Mine is for me and me only, you might want to share yours, help with the reflection process, but give yourself those five minutes. It's just about the amount of time it takes to make a decent cup of tea. Writing a journal also improves your communication skills and reduces anxiety and stress.

Having difficulty sleeping? No problem, write in your journal. Worrying about future tasks contributes significantly to peoples stress levels and increased stress levels leads to reduced sleep. It makes sense that brain dumping those worries into your journal greatly reduces your stress levels and… You sleep better! Did I mention that in one study, it showed that people who journaled, also fell asleep quicker than those people who didn't keep a journal.

I could go on. It helps boost your self esteem, improves creativity, helps you solve problems, regulates your mood and on and on it goes. There are a large number of books, Apps and journals out there. Do some research, figure out which one works for you and start writing. You'll be amazed at the results, I hope.

In any case, it's a great way to leave a record of your day for your future self and all for only five minutes a day.

STEP ASIDE, I'VE GOT THIS

Be confident

Adjective: confident
1. Feeling or showing confidence in oneself or one's abilities or qualities

I have confidence in sunshine
I have confidence in rain
I have confidence that spring will come again
Besides, which you see
I have confidence in me

Songwriter Richard Rodgers

If there was ever a word that screamed don't be a dick, this would be the word. I've met dozens, probably hundreds of people who, on first blush, you think... What a dick. Now it is true that some people are dicks, irrespective of their confidence level, they just are. Rich, poor, clever, dumb as a bag of frogs, fat, thin, tall, short and so on and so on, they are just dicks. Avoid these people at all costs. They are usually toxic and have their head so far up their own ass, they can't smell the bullshit that's wafting off them in large, toxic plumes. RUN THE FUCK AWAY! They need you in their lives way more than you need them.

"Sure, but what if one of these dicks is my boss, what do I do then, numb nuts?" I hear you ask, well, great fucking question, and the answer might not be something you want to hear, but I'm gonna tell you anyway, cos that's my job right here, right now. The answer is... change jobs (where you can). Listen, I know it's hard, I know it's difficult. You might have worked somewhere twenty years and some up and coming ass wipe sweeps in and busts your balls from day one. Chances are, if you've been there twenty years, you've seen this type of douchebag waft in and sweep out a thousand times, and if you think that's the case here, perhaps you just have to tough it out, but perhaps they are staying and there's fuck all you can do about it.

I get it, but you probably spend more time with the people you work with than your own family, that's a long time, and sometimes, you just gotta step away, but before you sail off into the sunset, flipping the bird to your new adversary, have the confidence to walk up to your boss and say hey, can I have a private word? Then, have the private word. Explain to your boss why you think you have to leave, tell them about the conflict, bullying, harassment, whatever it is. Better still keep a diary and every time dick stain says something out of line, write it in your book, when they said it and, if possible, why. Show that sucker to your boss and see what they do. I bet a pound to a pinch of salt, the pain in your ass will be gone, or out of your hair, very quickly. This should happen for a couple of reasons.

Hopefully your boss thinks shit, this person has worked here for twenty years, they have a great record and work super hard. I believe them, because they've never given me a reason to and I should support them.

If pain in the ass is a pain in the ass to you, chances are they are a pain in the ass to many others, you might just be the tip of the proverbial iceberg and they might even be a pain in the ass for your boss and they are just waiting for a reason to fire the son-of-a-bitch.

You're a nice person and even if you end up leaving, you deserve to be heard. Your voice is a valid one and is an important one. That's a very down example of confidence, but you get the idea. Shall we get on to a more confident example of what being confident means, because all this loosing your job talk is bumming me out!

Confidence.There is a misconception that ONLY confident people are confident. That may sound weird and wanky, but stick with me. If I ever do any public speaking, well NOW I love it, I know what I'm talking about and I'm confident I can hold my own, answer questions or even have the confidence to say I don't know the answer, but I'll find it out and pass it on as soon as is possible. Why can I do this now? Because I practiced, it's just like riding a bike. Think of the last person who won the tour de France, did they start out being able to beat everyone else in their class? No, of course not. They got a bike, eventually learned how to ride it, then rode it for a kilometre, then two, then five, then ten.... Public speaking is exactly the same (except you don't get as good looking calfs) You start in a classroom, in front of five people and you answer a question, then you get around to asking a question, then the group grows to ten people and five minutes, then twenty people and ten minutes and eventually you'll be talking to a stadium full of people, hanging on your every word. Now, you might still be shitting yourself inside, but outside, you will blind people with your confidence. There's an old saying we use in the forces "Bullshit with confidence" and from that bullshit will grow into real, actual confidence.

Confidence is a skill, it can be taught and it can be learned. You can start with none and develop it till you are a megastar. There are countless actors, musicians and performers who say, in real life, they are shy and don't have a lot of confidence, until they actually tell you that, you wouldn't believe it in a million years and you are confident. You do a thousand things a day with supreme confidence: Get out of bed in the morning, brush your teeth, have a shower, get dressed, make a coffee, drive or commute to work, actually navigate your working day, talk to venders and work colleagues and bosses and, fuck! you do a LOT in a day and you've developed every single one of those skills, you can develop skills in confidence too, unless you're Karen in HR, no one fucking likes you Karen, you're a snitch and I'm pretty sure you stole my yogurt out of the staffroom fridge last week, but screw you Karen, I'm lacing my yogurt with laxatives tomorrow, then we'll see who's right, whilst you shit yourself and I laugh my yogurt less ass off! I feel better for having gotten that off my chest!

Finally on this, if you really, really, REALLY want to give your confidence a shot in the arm, then check your local area for stand up comedy courses and sign yourself up immediately. It's terrifying, fun, funny and utterly brilliant. You'll be, if like me, shaking like a shitting dog, but you'll come out of your show, and you only have to do like a five minute set, like King fucking Kong! After that, talking to anyone is a piece of piss and your confidence will go stratospheric.

I'M GONNA DO THAT FOR SURE

Be dependable

adjective: dependable
Trustworthy and reliable

This one might only be a paragraph long, but I thought it was an important one to include, simply because I believe being dependable or, alternatively, not dependable will colour pretty much every single relationship you ever have. People will still love you if you're not dependable, like parents and siblings for example, but they won't trust you to deliver on something you've promised to deliver on. This, I guarantee, will make you feel pretty utterly shit, and we don't want that, do we?

There are only two words in the dictionary I use, to describe dependable: trustworthy and reliable. It's no more complicated than that. Do what you say you are going to do, and do it when you say you are going to say it. Now, if you say you're going to meet your mate Steve for a pint down the local in half an hour and you leave the house, fall over and break your arm, and you spend the next nine hours in ED, no one will blame you for standing them up, least of all Steve, but If you don't contact Steve the next day and tell him what happened, more than likely this will happen, you'll forget about Steve, until you bump into him twelve weeks later, after you've had your cast removed, in the same pub you should have met in twelve weeks earlier and then you tell him, he's gonna call bullshit and you're going to look like an idiot.e trustworthy, how? Tell the truth. Be honest, if you commit to something, see it through. Be on time, better still be early, fashionably early, not like four hours earlier, that's just weird.

You are responsible for you. Yes, shit happens and plans go awry, and that's perfectly acceptable, but keep everyone informed, as best you can. Trust is incredibly fragile and fickle and can be broken with a single word, action or look. Do your very best not to break it, because once it's broken, it's like a plate. You can fix it, but it will never be the same afterwards and it will never be as strong as it was before you broke it.

Equally, if people perceive you as not reliable, or worse actually unreliable (Someone who's consistently unreliable, as opposed to periodically unreliable), That's something that's really hard to get back once you're labelled unreliable.

COME ON KID, YOU CAN DO IT

Become the voice of encouragement
verb: encourage; 3rd person present: encourages; past tense: encouraged; past participle: encouraged; gerund or present participle: encouraging
Give support, confidence, or hope to (someone).

It's SO easy to knock someone down. Damage their confidence, bruise their ego. We've built an entire society on it I think, sometimes, but to actively encourage someone is to give them a remarkable gift.

My wife shared with me a letter a Principal of a school in Singapore sent to the parents of their pupils prior to an exam. I can't credit the Principal, no details were available from the post, but if you are that Principal, or you know who they are, just let them know they are remarkable and absolutely understand how to encourage students and their families alike.

Dear Parents, The exams your children are about to start soon. I know you are really anxious for your children to do well.
But, please remember, amongst the students who will be sitting for the exams there is an artist, who doesn't need to understand maths,… There is an entrepreneur, who doesn't care about History or English Literature… There is a musician, who's chemistry marks won't matter… There's an athlete… who's physical fitness is more important than physics… If your child does get top marks, that's great! But if he or she doesn't… please don't take away their self-confidence and dignity from them. Tell them it's OK, it's just an exam. They are cut out for much bigger things in life. Tell them, no matter what they score… Tell them that you love them and will not judge them. Somebody give that teacher a rise!

Give support, confidence or hope. What three wonderful, warm and caring words. Confidence we've already covered previously, but support, it can be a smile, a nod of the head, a pat on the back, a kind word, a reassuring nudge in the right direction. We all need encouragement from time to time, even those of us who are considered confident and 'together' and the thing is, we all know how to encourage. It's around us constantly. You might not have been directly in its line of fire, you might have grown up in a fractured household, with people who had profound difficulty showing any kind of emotion. You might have been in foster homes, or felt disconnected to your family, but I guarantee you saw it on TV, in a movie, heard it in the words of a song, or read it in the words of a book. We might just chose not to 'offer' it, you know when sometimes you wake up in a foul mood, and you're just like,

"No, fuck you world, I'm not playing today".

You know, like that kind of thing. There's no way you're going to be encouraging people on days like that, that's a good day to stay in doors and away from people all together, but just in a general kind of way, try to be more encouraging, more positive and helpful.

If you already do this, I encourage you to continue. See, even I can get in on the action.

HUMILITY IS HUMBLING.

adjective
adjective: humble; comparative   adjective: humbler; superlative adjective: humblest
1. 1.
Having or showing a modest or low estimate of one's importance.

Humility is a strange fish to fry, on one hand I want you to own your achievements and be confident in your decisions, at the same time, I don't want you being an arrogant ass hat.

I guess the easiest way to skirt around this is to do a comparison of a situation.

You've achieved something. Doesn't matter what it is, you made a big sale at work, whatever, you figure out what it is. Your boss comes in, holding the weekly sales report with a big, shit kicking grin on their face.

Scenario #1
Boss "Hey people, the sales reports have come in for the week, and you're killing it. Who made the McDonald sale?"
You "Yeah, hey boss. Did you see that big sale yesterday, I did that. I sold those things"

Congratulations, you're an ass hat and everyone hates you.

Scenario #2
Boss "Hey people, sales reports have come in for the week, and you're killing it. Who made
        the McDonald sale"?

You "Yeah, I closed that one boss, with a bit of help from these work shites."

Okay. Confident, but not too braggy. You kept it together.

Scenario #3

Boss "Hey people, sales reports have come in for the week, and you're killing it. Who made the McDonald sale"?

You "Yeah, I closed that one, but everyone had a hand in it boss. Jenny, Geoff, Colin. I think it was Sandra's coffee that closed the deal."

You're a humble team player who looks out for their coworkers-Aced it!

You tell me. Which one makes you appear confident? Which one shows you as a humble team player, who's team supports them? And which one was a complete and utter dick? All three had the same outcome, but you came off way better in one of them because you showed a little humility. It didn't diminish from what you achieved, in fact it highlighted what you achieved, whilst simultaneously putting you in the good books of every single person you work with AND showed your boss what a bad ass team player you are. Showing humility does not mean you are weak, in fact the opposite happens. It shows a degree of modesty, and that's a very powerful power to have.

Sure, take credit, when credit is due, but wait for it to come up. Self praise is no praise at all and the 'Look at me' philosophy is a very ugly philosophy to adopt, and people see through that shallow venire very, very easily. Being humble grounds you, makes you more approachable, accessible. People want to work with you, and if you have the confidence to back up that humility, people will listen to you and follow you too.

Apply this to any situation, with any type of person-family, friends, boss, co-workers, strangers, anyone, but especially yourself, and it just makes for a much nicer journey through this life. You'll enjoy all the successes just as much, it just won't be quite as bumpy a journey.

TWO SUGARS PLEASE

Buy a homeless person a coffee

I currently live in Australia. I've lived here with my family since around 2006. I'm a proud, card carrying, flag waving Australian, with an Australian passport. I LOVE my adoptive country, it has been very, very good to me, and yet…. At the time of writing this, Australia had a population of around 27 million, that's in a country the size of North America. We have a very small population and yet we have huge problems with poverty and homelessness. I do NOT want to get political, but in a country this size, with the population we have, there should be no poverty and no homelessness, it's just unacceptable. Now some people have mental health issues, some choose to be homeless, but for the vast majority of homeless, and it's just a hunch, I think don't actually want to be homeless.

Same with poverty, true poverty. I've heard stories of young girls having to use used socks stuffed with tissue paper to produce make-shift tampons, because they couldn't afford to buy any. Birth control, sanitary products and mental health medication should be given free to all those that seek them. It's only recently, for Gods sake, that GST was removed from sanitary products! What makes a sanitary towel a fucking luxury item? The government, irrespective of who's in charge, have to be held accountable. In fact, you know who's in charge? YOU! You vote them in, you vote them out. They aren't doing what you want them to do, remove them! They'll soon get the idea.

Anyway, I don't know what the answer is, well not all of it, and because I don't know the answer, I do what I can, give some to charity, but I'm always convinced most charities skim off the top most of the money they maker is donated, due to 'administrative fees' whatever the fuck they are, so I'm generally reluctant, unless there's a disclaimer saying 99.9% of all money raised goes directly to whoever I'm giving it to. What I can do is something I've been doing every time I go into the city for as long as I can remember, I guy someone who's homeless, a cup of coffee and some food.

Don't go trying to get me Sainted just yet. It's a cup of coffee and some food, usually from a 7/11, so I'm talking $5 max? I do this for a couple of reasons, firstly, I'm never too sure if someone's just gonna buy booze or drugs, but really, who gives a fuck? If I was homeless, I'd want a drink, or to get off my face too, but I think the person I stumble upon might benefit from a coffee and some food more, I don't know. Secondly, it gives me a chance to say Hi, have a little chat to 'em. You have to pick your person, but I've yet to have a conversation I didn't like and for the love of God, I bet you a million bucks, most of those poor souls spend almost all of the day being ignored or moved on. Whenever I chat, they are always grateful, remember to take lots of sugar sachets with you, and they've usually got something interesting to say, you just have to be prepared to listen. I know I've mentioned this a couple of times, and I could have edited it out, but I think it's really important to repeat and hopefully, get you engages in doing it. I don't mention it out of vanity, I mention it out of hope.

When I was 15 I got kicked out of my house-evil step father, that kind of story. I lived in Manchester and thought the streets of London are paved with gold. I'll go there, make my fortune and show everyone they were wrong about me. I got to London, the streets were not paved with gold and I became homeless.

The place I slept was in the doorway of a shop called The Tie Rack, in Victoria train Station. I'd bed down about 10PM and get kicked out, so the cleaners could clean around 4AM. I'd go to the toilet, brush my teeth, wash my face and head off into the cold London mornings. I had a back pack, so I just looked like a tourist. I'd head to this shop I knew that had bread delivered and steal a loaf of bread, or some Bagels (Sorry shop) Then I'd head to Kensington, or similar and steal a bottle of milk from a couple of door steps, not two milk from a single house, I wasn't a monster! (Sorry home owners) But, I did what I had to do to survive. I'd then spend the day going to as many free places as I could. The V&A, The National Portrait Gallery, The British Library, The Museum of Natural Sciences. Endless places, filled with magic and wonder and education, I think it was the best education I could have ever received. I lived like that for six months. Six months being homeless and alone and 15, not even an adult! I would have died for a decent conversation with someone who didn't look down on me. Not once in all that time did someone try to prostitute me, fuck me, drug me or beat me. I was completely and utterly alone, and if I can spare one person that loneliness, even for five minutes, a few times a year, it's money and time well spent.

Now, imagine if everyone did that? Everyone who went into the city, or worked in the city, went out of their way, for ten minutes, to buy someone a coffee and a sausage roll and gave someone five minutes of their time for a quick chat. How much better to you think you'd feel if you did that? How much better do you think the homeless person would feel? Imagine if, for once, they felt some self worth and that was the spark that turned them around, got them thinking, got them moving. What if they sort help, cleaned themselves up, found sheltered accommodation, started selling The Big Issue and had some self worth for once? Imagine a world like that. Yes, I know it wouldn't work for everyone, but fuck it, imagine if it worked for 10% of the homeless! That's still fucking massive. That cup of coffee will have virtually no impact on you, your budget or your day. If you just buy the coffee it's literally $1, but the impact it will have on the person you're giving it to will be unmeasurable. Besides, you'll get a warm 'n' fuzzy feeling inside when you help your fellow man, it will help to cleanse your soul.

So buy someone a coffee and a sandwich, I beg you on the homeless person's behalf and buy a copy of The Big Issue. It genuinely affects those selling it and it's a really great read.

On a side note, I just wanted you guys to know that the last time we went into Melbourne, my youngest asked me if it would be okay if she bought a homeless person a cup of coffee and a sandwich too! Fucking SCORE!

REMAIN OR BECOME OPEN MINDED

adjective
adjective: open-minded; adjective: openminded
1. Willing to consider new ideas; unprejudiced.

I AM open-minded, I hear you scream into the open pages of this book, but are you… really? It takes around 12 weeks, as already mentioned, for your brain to form and consolidate new neurological pathways, so chances are most of your thought pathways are already locked in. In fact most of your internal processes are either genetic, meaning you were built with them, or soaked up, like a sponge, by the time you hit puberty. A lot of that shit is hard wired into your DNA and it's not an easy task to either remain, or become, open-minded.

Let's take a heavy hitter, let's, as best we can in a book like this, cover something like racism. Racism, for me, is one of the most hateful crimes against our fellow man that there is. Now don't get me wrong, I'll happily despise someone if they're an asshole, or hateful in anyway, but to hate someone for the colour of their skin? That just doesn't make any fucking sense to me! And yes, that goes both ways, I've seen plenty of people of colour hate on white people too, the river flows both ways, but white people hating on everyone else, that's the strongest fucking river there is and if you're reading this and you are a racist, then fuck you, you're a dumb ass idiot and you should be ashamed of yourself, and do better!

Now I'm a white, middle aged, middle income man, I know almost fuck all about racism, but what I do know is that we are not born with it, we are taught it, we are exposed to it and we 'learn' that it is 'normal', but here's the thing, it's not normal, it's far from normal, it's close-minded, not surprisingly, the polar opposite of open-minded! There is a point however when what you've been taught turns into what you think, or believe. It's at this point you make a choice, you remain a racist motherfucker, or you better yourself. You can change, you are allowed, it is possible. Now I'm not just talking about racism here, obviously, I'm talking about whatever it is that's blocking you from being the best version of yourself. It might be religion, politics, how you feel about Uncle Pete, or Karen from HR!

Now you might be the most open-minded person to have ever walked the face of this little blue ball in space, and if you are, I commend you and thank you for your forward thinking, progressive attitude, in which case, just skip the rest of this chapter and move along, but, you might be the kind of person who's got a little way to go. As I've mentioned before, I've been a Registered General Nurse for almost thirty years, thirty fucking years! And during that time I've worked with thousands of people from all over the world and I've universally liked the nice people, despised the dicks and not once did race come into that equation. So how do you remove racism? Well, I'm going to bastardise a quote I read once that read:

"How do you get rid of racism? Instead of saying A black thief was pursued by a white cop, just say a thief was pursued by a cop"

Race and racial identity is important, but that's not JUST who you are, it's part of you for sure, but it shouldn't define you, any more than your sexuality, shoe size or colour of your hair and it definitely shouldn't have any baring on how you define someone else, be smarter than that, look deeper than that, BE better than that.

Remain open-minded! If you're not sure if you are a racist or not, if you think every person of colour is from the "Hood," every Indian likes curry, every Arab drives a taxi, or every white guy is a button down, nerdy accountant who only eats egg and chips, or, every Asian knows Kung Fu! Read that last sentence again and please, for the love of God! Recognise the absurdity of it, it's fucking mental, if you think like that, then you need to know it's stereotyping and you are a racist and completely inaccurate and you need to adjust your attitude accordingly and likewise, if you're not that person, but you know who that person is, you have a moral obligation to speak up and put that shit down. Silence, in the face of racism, is guilt by omission or denial, you have to speak up. You have to make the person saying hateful things feel very, very uncomfortable. Uncomfortable enough to make them stop, BUT to realise WHY they need to stop. If they do not possess the skills to be self enlightened, you enlighten them.

Phew!

Look at me, being all mister human rights, like I know what it's like to face this shit. I don't, obviously, Well, I do have to put up with a lot of Irish jokes (Still racist) but, in all seriousness, I hope I can at the very least elicit change, or a dialogue to some small degree.

It's safe to say I kind of just ran with that, but let's open this discussion up a bit beyond that, shall we? We are talking, in general terms, about becoming, or remaining, open-minded. If you are open-minded, then congratulations, I am proud of you. Pass on your philosophy to everyone you know and move through like unburdened from such restraints. If, however, you've not quite there yet, we may need to do some work.

Now being open minded doesn't always mean you have to change your mind, it just means you have to be willing to hear someone else's mind, for a moment or two, assess what you've heard and act accordingly. You may believe the Earth is round, a flat Earther believes, not surprisingly, that the world is flat! If you're talking to someone with this belief, be courteous enough to at least hear their rational behind their beliefs. After you've heard what they have to say, either change what you believe, or continue to believe the world is round. Then never talk to that lunatic again! No, only joking, don't do that.

In reality, it doesn't matter what you're talking about, it could be heavy hitters; religion, politics, parental advise, whatever. What matters is that you are prepared to enter into a conversation with as open a mind as possible. Now it may be that you're belief system is set in stone, I for example, 100% don't believe in the physical punishment of children, institutionally (The Caine, for example) Or domestically (Getting 'The Belt'). The thought of a child being deliberately harmed makes me feel sick to my stomach, especially as I was physically abused as a kid myself, but what if someone who does believe in to talks to you on the subject;

"I'd never normally hit my child…"
First of all, anyone who says that, is a fucking liar, they hit their kids all the fucking time, they just choose to 'justified' their actions.
"… But little Tommy ran out into the Road yesterday and almost got run over. Like a car literally just missed him. I smacked his bottom, because

he had to understand there could have been real, devastating consequences to his actions".

What do you do with that one? How do you unwrap that nugget? Truth is, I kinda get what that person is saying. I fundamentally standby my philosophy on the subject?

DO NOT HIT YOUR FUCKING KIDS!

"It's been shown in clinical studies, that corporal punishment simply does not work. You can't punish out bad behaviour and, in fact, physical punishment can lead to increased aggression, antisocial behaviour, obviously physical injury and mental health problems, yet in America alone, it is estimated that two-thirds of Americans still approved of spanking their kids".

This is made all the more tricky because I know, from first hand experience, that one of the things most parents hate, is being told how to parent, by other parents! You're just as likely to get a "Go fuck yourself" and mind your own business, as you are, okay let's have a debate about that!

Ultimately, you have to be prepared to listen to the other side of the coin, argue your point if you must, agree or disagree with the other persons point of view and move on. If the opposing philosophy is so far removed from your starting point that you don't kink you'll ever find a common ground, then don't, that's fine too. Just say you'll have to agree to disagree and move on from there, if you can. At other times, the strongest thing you can do is to just walk away. Walk away from the conversation, or walk away from the friend, family member or co-worker and let them live their lives, whilst you get on living yours.

Sometimes, however, you just have to forget all about racist, misogynistic, homophobic, bigoted Uncle Donald, because no one likes him and just get on with your life.

YES! THEY SAID NO

Change your perspective on failure
noun: failure
1. 1.
    Lack of success

Okay, this one is really quick and it's in the form of a short fable.

You are trying to sell something and you only have one of them. You know it's sellable, but you just need ONE sale. You walk into a room with one hundred people and start asking who'd like to buy your item. The first person says no, they are not interested. GOOD! That's great news. It's great for a couple of reasons. Firstly, if that person doesn't want your product, then they clearly not the person who should be buying it. You just need one yes, and that no just got you one step closer to getting it. That no just became a win.

It's a difficult idea to wrap your head around at first, but once you get it, it's a game changer. That NO just got you one step closer to your YES. Tricky thing is, what happens if you go through that entire room and 100 people say no, what do you do then? You change rooms! And if you're about to go into that room and you're not 100% committed to that product, they will smell it a mile off. Remember people buy people, not products. You believe it, they will believe it, and how do you make sure you remain positive and confident? For me, I remember the film Sharknado! The producer of Sharknado follows me on Twitter, something I'm profoundly proud of, but what I absolutely love about Sharknado, is that someone went into a pitch meeting with a bunch of executive producers and pitched and SOLD a story about a tornado with killer sharks in it. Someone wrote the script, someone green lit the project, someone funded it, someone filmed it, and someone sold it and it made the makers millions and millions of dollars and spawned at least FIVE sequels! That is bat shit crazy and bonkers and utterly brilliant and a wonderful example of how to change your perspective on failure. A no is not a failure, it's just a no from that one person you asked. There is a yes out there, there always is. It might take you a while to find it, you just have to have the confidence to keep asking the question,

BACK OF THE NET

Have a goal
noun
noun: goal; plural noun: goals
2. The object of a person's ambition or effort; an aim or desired result.

One way of guaranteeing you don't reach your destination, is to not to actually have a goal in the first place. Think about what you want to achieve and give yourself a realistic time frame by which to achieve it. No point saying I'm going to lose 40Kg in three months, unless you're having surgery, in which case you might actually manage it, but if you're not having surgery, you are setting yourself up to fail, then you'll fail, then you'll feel crappy about it, fall off the diet bandwagon and need to lose 44Kg next time around. But what if you say my goal is to lose 0.5 kg a week consistently and incorporate some modest exercise into my normal daily routine. That seems like a much more attainable goal, doesn't it? It might take a little longer, but it's a damned site shorter than waiting those 12 weeks and losing nothing except your desire to continue on your weight loss plan.

Pick a start date and stick to it. There's a saying that goes, the hardest part about going to the gym is putting your trainers on, and I think this is true. You put the trainers on and mentally, you've already committed to going. So part of having a goal, is having a plan and sticking to it.

How do you break a goal down? Well, for me, I have short term goals, intermediate goals and long term goals. A short term goal might be; send that email I had to respond to, get dinner prepared early, if you're really down, it might just be get out of bed and take a shower. These are your goals, things you want to achieve. With that in mind, it's really important that, as the crazy kids say today, "You do you". Your goals have to be your goals. Don't manifest a goal because it's something you think your partner, or significant other, might want. Don't do it for your boss or your kids or your mother, set the goals for you. You are that important. This list should be forever growing and shrinking as you achieve your goals and subsequently build new ones. It's also very important to recognise that you are infallible, you will make mistakes and you will fail. The significant thing to focus on moments like this is to allow yourself the luxury of failure, recognise it, forgive yourself, reset, or redefine your goals and move forward without being weighed down by the weight of that particular 'failure'. Just remember all those self made millionaires who failed several times before they found their stride.

Intermediate goals are those goals that can take two months or two years. Next year I'm going to go backpacking for six months, how am I going to do that? I'm gonna loose 30 kg by Christmas next year, I've going to finish school or write my book, or take a class on portrait painting and paint my first portrait. Remember, you set the goals, you set the timetable, you are in charge. I believe it was Einstein who said the definition of insanity was doing the same thing over and over again and expecting different outcomes. If you've done nothing to change your future, why would your future change? Simple answer is that it won't. You'll be on that same old, boring treadmill until you drop down dead, having achieved none of your goals.

You can, of course, combine goals, short and intermediate goals, intermediate and long term goals. In five years I want my PhD. To get there, I need to take these classes at College, and then these subjects at University.

I want to be the head of my own department by the time I reach 40. To do that, I have to follow these short term career pathways. Or I want to open my second shop, again, it doesn't matter what the goals are (to me), I could guess for the next thousand years and never get it. These are your goals, set by you, for you.

You might not even have any goals! Is that possible? Well, of course it is. There are plenty of people out there who punch in every morning and punch out every night and the thought of their 'normal' routine being disrupted by any kind of aspiration, utterly appalls them. My brother had the same job for thirty years, did he have a goal? In relation to his work, no, clearly he didn't. His goal was to work hard enough that he could afford to take his next vacation. His annual holiday was his goal. Simple, unambiguous, stress free. Earn enough money that I can go on holiday and not worry about how much I'm spending. Is my brother any less happy for not having more lofty goals? Hell no, he's totally chill and stress free, likewise I have friends who have a clearly defined trajectory and they are sticking to it and the knowledge that they have those goals in place offers them a huge amount of comfort. The trouble arises when your goals don't match either your aspirations, or your abilities. I may very well aspire to be the next Captain of the Starship Enterprise, do I possess the ability to do that? Of course I don't, are you mad! 1. It doesn't fucking exist (In real life) and 2. I'm too old and fat and knackered, BUT could I write a book about the Captain of a Star Ship, who goes out, into the great unknown of space and has many wild and fanciful adventures? Damn straight I could do that. Would that not then make me the Captain of my own ship? Hell yes it would! See, it's perception Vs effort divided by ability.

You strive, you thrive (I just made that up and I'm quite pleased with myself). What I mean by that is, if you don't have a dream, a goal, something to work towards, you stop. You stagnate, you wither and, eventually, you die. Well, we all die, but would you rather die having packed your life to the brim, stuffed with the journey of a thousand goals, or would you rather die having never tried to reach beyond your grasp? One is not necessarily better than the other, but I know which one I'd choose to live. If you don't want that, then that perfectly fine too. Like I've said before, this is your life and you have to live it as you see fit. I can show you the options, you chose both the journey and the destination. Go wild, you might just end up surprising yourself.

I'M GONNA PASS

Fidelity is a great thing
noun: fidelity
1.
Faithfulness to a person, cause, or belief, demonstrated by continuing loyalty and support.

At the time of writing this, I am 55 years old. I will have been with my wife for almost 30 years and I cannot imagine being with anyone else, in fact the mere thought of thinking about being with someone else both appalls me and fills me with dread, even if it was Mary Stuart Masterson from the 1987, Howard Deutch film Some Kind Of Wonderful. I loved you then, I love you still! Luckily, no one else could tolerate me quite the way my wife does, I'm a fucking nightmare and anyone else would stick a breadknife in my chest for being such a pain in the ass, thank God my wife doesn't know where the bread knife is kept!

I have friends who are on 'dating' sites and they regularly hook up with other people on the same sites, you know how they work, but are they 'dating' sites? If the person you're meeting is called 'Hot69,' I'm gonna say no, it's not a dating site, it's a shagging site and ALL of my friends confirm this. You go in, shag and leave. You might never know the persons actual name! You might only know you shagged with someone called Hot69, which for me, is hilarious and inconceivable. Just the thought of how many STD's you could get alone is mind boggling to me. At least the male/female ones, the women are a little more discerning (I hope), for gay sites, I'm informed, you just need the other person to have a cock and a pulse hahaha. Men, it turns out, don't necessarily care about what they're doing, as long as they are doing something, and their dick is in something, anything, doesn't matter! I bet that's a revelation!

In this instance, of course, I'm talking about sexual fidelity and it is way, way, way too underrated. I am religious, I do have faith and my marriage vows are, for me and my wife, a solum commitment in the presence of God. You may not feel the same. You might have gotten married, I don't know, on a beach and have no faith to talk of. The idea of infidelity might even excite you! If you're both into that kind of thing, all power to you. If you can make that work, then you can make that work.

There's a growing body of people who believe 'we' as a society, are not designed for a monogamous relationship. We are designed, by nature, to have as many partners as we can catch. There are some religions, for example, that actively encourage men to have multiple wives. Not the women you understand, the women can't have multiple husbands, funny that! I am a flawed human being, and ultimately I can attest to knowing very little, but one thing I do know is, if you're married, don't fuck around, or fuck around and don't be married, or be honest about it. IF you're both fucking around and you're cool with it, then like I said, all power to you. If you're swingers or a cuckhold (Not quite sure what that is, but I heard it in a TV show, so it has to be a real thing, then great, have fun. Just don't lie about it, don't cheat. It does nothing but hurt those you probably profess to love.

Okay, that's being faithful in the context of a loving, singular partnership, but there are obviously many different types of fidelity. A dog can be faithful to their owner for example, although I can't ask you to emulate that, so it's not a great example. Best friends can be faithful to their relationship. So it's all about being faithful to a person, a cause or belief. You can be faithful to your religion, to your football team, to your political party. You can be the faithful follower of a TV series (Mine is Star Trek! I'm talking meeting the cast, watching every episode of every show, ever, multiple times, going to conventions, collecting props. The whole seven of nine yards! Little Star Trek joke in there for ya. I am very faithful to that show and that show has taught me many valuable lessons. You know, that kind of faithful)

One of the things about faith is, no one can give it to you. You have to believe in it, whatever iteration of faith you're dealing with. No one can tell you to develop faith in something, no one can force or coheres you into it, except for cults, brainwashing, blood sucking cults, you gotta watch those slippery bastards, but generally speaking, it has to come from you, from within. I am a Roman Catholic and I have friends who hear about my religion and say I don't believe in all that mumbo-jumbo bullshit. That's fine, that's why it's called faith and not fact! You have to take that leap of faith, to have faith. Paradoxical, but true. It's also worth making a little mental note, to remind yourself, that no one can force what they believe on you, any more than you can do the same to then.

The last thing I'll say on this is that you have to remember, if we are talking about loving someone, that there is a person on the other end of this equation. There is someone who is hopefully loving you in return. They have opened up their hearts to you and you alone and all they expect is the same in return. If you can't do that, then perhaps you have to reconsider if you're the type of person who should be in a monogamous relationship?Not everyone should be.

NB. The Internet states that:

A cuckold is the husband of an adulterous wife, ie A cuckhold watches his wife have sex with someone else; the wife of an adulterous husband is a Cuckqueen.

DON'T B FLAT PLEASE

Sing and dance

I'm not going to provide a dictionary definition of singing or fucking dancing here today, I know for a fact that even if you have never done either of these activities, you know what they are, but do you know why you should be doing them? That's the question.

Let's start with singing.

Well, turns out, irrespective of wether or not you can carry a tune, there is solid scientific evidence to prove singing is both good for your body and mental health.

Relieves Stress. Well, duh! Show me a good show tune that doesn't. Oh, you want like, actual fact type things? Okay. In a 2017 study, scientists measures the amount of Cortisol, the stress hormone to you and me, in people's saliva before and after they sang and guess what? Yep, the hormone was reduced after singing. It only works if you're singing somewhere where you're not stressed to begin with, like in the bath. If someone pushed you out onto a stage at the Royal Albert Hall to sing, your stress hormone would fly out of the fucking roof! Unless you're actually used to singing at the Royal Albert Hall, in which case, go you.

2. Stimulates the immune response. Yes, singing increases a person's immunoglobulin A levels, increasing a persons immune system.

3. It kind of goes without saying that singing can significantly improve lung function. It's worth noting singing doesn't treat or cure ailments or conditions. Singing New York, New York won't cure your Asthma, but your respiratory muscles will strengthen and that will have some associated benefits. It also helps with conditions like cystic fibrosis, MS, asthma and Chronic Obstructive Pulmonary Disorder (COPD). It also increases the amount of oxygen in your blood and this helps to both improve your pulmonary system and has the added benefit of improving mood, think those hormones again, and (If you're singing in a group) an increased sense of belonging.

4. Enhances memory in people with dementia. This one is, in my humble opinion, quite remarkable. People with, predominantly Alzheimer's disease, but other types of dementia, have been found to be able to recall song lyrics, long after they've forgotten everything else in their lives. The thing is, that whilst these people were able to recall these songs, if the songs they were recalling were learned in that person's childhood, the singing of that song would result in the spontaneous return of auto biological details for many, many people. It really is quite amazing.

There are many, many other benefits. Too many to list here, but singing improves mood, if singing in a choir, gives you a sense of belonging, can improve symptoms of snoring and if you manage to throw playing a wind instrument in there too, you've just increased the chances of helping with obstructive sleep apnea (OSA). The internet is literally littered with articles, studies and research backing all of this up, but if you decide I'm talking a load of bollocks (I'm not) and you want to focus on just one thing, focus on this; No one can sing a song and feel like shit, unless you're at a funeral or something, but mostly, singing is great for you, so get your toes tapping, get your fingers clicking, turn the volume up on whatever you listen to music on and sing your ass off, until you can't sing any more. You will feel awesome for it!

Dance baby, dance.

This one is nowhere near as scientific as singing. Singing was like a damned lecture. I had to look up big words and everything! Dancing, by comparison, is a cake walk.

Have you ever been to a wedding, or a birthday party and the DJ drops a beat you can't help but dance to? And you jump up, like your chair's been electrified and you leap to the dance floor, dragging everyone else along for the ride, as you subsequently dance your ass off for the next twenty minutes and eventually, when you stop, you're absolutely knackered? We all know that right?

By the end of that night, assuming you do that quite a few more times, you've inadvertently improved the condition of your heart and lungs. You've increased muscular strength, endurance and motor fitness.

You've increased your aerobic fitness, muscle tone and strength. You'll be more agile and flexible (your partner's going to thank you big time for that one) and you will be in a better general condition. You will have reduced your risk of osteoporosis, improved your coordination AND significantly improved any weight management program you might be on!

What do you mean, you want more!

It helps beat depression, can boost your memory, reduces stress and helps you develop and/or maintain your core strength and body balance.

Now, imagine you're home alone. You've done the school run and the kids are out. You shipped your partner off to work this morning, they are gone for the day. The house is silent, there are no witnesses, no one to shout out 'Shame' and point at you and laugh. There are absolutely NO negative consequences associated with what you are about to do. You stand, in the middle of your living area and think hard, and then it comes to you, perhaps you've always known, but you find yourself telling your home device to play your favourite tune and to crank the volume up to ten. You wait for the track to be, first, selected and then… it starts to play! You go wild with excitement. You sing and dance around the living room to your favourite tune with not one single fuck to give. At the end, you are hot, sweaty and red faced, you're panting, perhaps even shacking a little. You are ALIVE and it feels wonderful. Now imagine doing that every day.

I DON'T WANT TO PUT IT IN THERE

If it feels wrong, don't fucking do it

We have become, in my opinion, somewhat morally ambiguous in recent years. We usually know what's right and wrong, don't we? But invariably what happens is, we just don't listen to our inner voice. The lines are blurred and we have no clear path to follow. Media, including both regular outlets and social media have muddied the waters to such an extent, that people are now confused (to a point) about what is right and what is wrong. What is acceptable and what is unacceptable, but there are many, many others who know what is acceptable, but make a conscious decision to just do what's right for them. To do what is easier, to follow the path of least resistance, to do what provides them the greatest profit, be that financial, emotional, physical.

You might be married, but it's gonna feel really good to shag that girl who's been smiling at me all night from across the bar.

You might disagree fundamentally with a proposal your boss is floating, but you're not gonna say anything. Why should you put yourself in their firing line, better to let someone else take the fall?

You really shouldn't take those steroids, that guy down the gym is offering you, but you want results, and you want them fast. No point in taking months to get the results you want, when you could do it in weeks.

A thousand reasons, a thousand excuses. We've all been there, we've all done it. We've all heard that nagging little voice in the back of our heads and we've equally all told that voice to go fuck itself, or pretended not to hear it in the first place, but if you sleep with that woman, bury your head in the sand, or take those drugs, just this one time, who are you really hurting? Well, on a singular level, you're hurting yourself. You may not have that much moral fibre left, but what there is could be disintegrating, like rotten cotton with every breath you take. You could be destroying relationships, yours with your wife, your kids, your extended family, your bosses, your co-workers, the girls relationship with her partner. The bonds of friendship might be stretched to snapping point because you keep putting your friends under enormous pressure to lie for you. You might be putting your career at risk, perhaps your boss needed someone to step up and confirm what they think is true, their idea sucks. They might be looking for someone to step up, take the reins and lead the department forward, because secretly, they've taken a promotion. You might put your heart under remarkable physical pressure, pressure enough to cause it to falter, flutter, perhaps even stop! There are a million things that can go wrong, with a million different decisions you make. You might always be on a path, irrespective of what you do, of hurting someone you love, respect or care about. The one thing you can say with absolute certainty however is this, you know, in that moment, how the decision you are about to make will make you feel. If it feels wrong, don't do it, because I promise you, if it feels wrong, it's gonna be wrong and you already know that. You might never want to say it, to yourself or anyone else, but you'll know it's wrong.

I can only offer this advice to someone who still retains a degree of moral fortitude. These words will fall flat on the serial cheater, or the career criminal or the dirty politician, or the bent cop, or any one of the myriad of cliched tropes. Please don't be that pedestrian, that predictable, that boring.

Let me be the first to say, I am in no position to take the moral high ground here, I'm not telling you what to do for a couple of reasons. Firstly, it's not my place to tell you what to do, only advise that sometimes there are alternative paths to take and you might feel a lot better about yourself if you take one of those, and secondly I know you already know the answer. The world is imperfect, and it is filled with imperfect things and people and we make a million poor decisions every single day, if we didn't there wouldn't be any crime or wars or poverty, there'd be no prejudice, racism or crimes against those who have a different religious belief or sexual orientation, things like that. I'm not suggesting you repent your mortal sins and follow a path of purity and enlightenment, although that sounds cool.

I know, on a global level, I'm asking for the brass ring and we might only get 50% of the way there, but can you imagine how better the world would be if we all managed to become 50% better than who we are right now? It is a big ask, but why not? Why not ask the big ask? On a personal level, it absolutely will make a different. A profound and almost instant difference, because you will be at peace with yourself, calm and stronger and more confident. Do one thing, just one. Do one thing right today that you normally wouldn't do, then tomorrow, do it again tomorrow and this time, add something else to it, you get the idea. It might be a life changing experience, but you'll never know if you don't give it a try.

I AIN'T DOIN' IT FOR YOU BABY

Don't be a people pleaser

I'll expand on that slightly, please don't be a people pleaser, be a person pleaser and, just incase you're not too sure who that someone should be, it's you dumb ass! You are a long time dead and you'll reach the grave exhausted if you try and please everyone, all of the time. Besides, who really thinks that's possible? What if you're faced with two people and each has a fundamentally different belief in relation to something you've said, done, felt or God forbid, one of your core beliefs? Three people need pleasing in that scenario, which one are you going to choose? I'll tell you exactly which one you'll choose, you'll choose the one in the middle. You'll choose you. You have to, what's the alternative? I'm not talking some stupid, narcissistic dick wad, who doesn't see, believe or act on behalf of anyone other than themselves. I'm talking about being self aware. I'm talking about taking your own feelings, thoughts, beliefs and again, God forbid wants, into consideration when you're deciding about something.

Now you may go for the 'Spock' approach where the "Needs of the many outweigh the needs of the few, or the one". Collectively, as a group, your friends want to go to a specific club after work, you don't. So what are your choices? SO simple: Go with the flow and get your groove on, or don't. Now there's nothing wrong with you saying "I'm not a massive fan of that place, their beer's watered down" Whatever, and if the group discuss that and ultimately decide to go with their original plan, that's fine. You said your piece, you moved on and you start to get your head around the fact you're going. You may have not gotten the result you wanted, but you spoke out for yourself, you were your own advocate and irrespective of the outcome, you will, I guarantee it, feel better for having aired your opinion, rather than stem it, shove it back into the shadows, never to be heard of again. Equally, several people in the group might have said, you know what, the beer is actually shite in that place, how about so and so? In which case, you changed everything with one sentence! You're a God damned superhero!

You know Geoff, in that other department? The one who always agrees with the boss and is a total suck up and everyone hates him, and more over, no one trusts him? He's a people pleaser and whilst that might get him so far, wit, ingenuity, gaul, the ability to speak your own mind succinctly, clearly and with reason, having faith in your own instincts and still be open to change and compromise, all of that is SO much more than Geoff will ever be, and you know what, his superiors know that too.

Being a person pleaser takes time, effort and commitment. We are, to a greater or lesser degree, programmed to be yes people. It makes for an easy life (for some) and it takes great effort and self awareness to stand up, speak out and ultimately, be strong to and for yourself. There will be many people who won't like or appreciate your free thinking approach, most of them will be called Geoff, (Geoff) and Karen! But you're not living your life for Geoff and Karen, well at least I hope you're not. You're living your life for you. You are your Northern star. You are your constant, the 'thing' that is always there when everyone and everything else has left and it's vital that you take care of yourself. You do you first. Do things for the right reason. Do things because you believe in them, not because someone else has told you their idea is cool.

All of that being said, there are a few exceptions to this rule. For example, you might decide following the law of the land isn't for you. You might want to go off and rob a bank, or murder someone (My money is on either Geoff and/or Karen), but you can't do those things, why? Because they are against the law, and you will be shot and/or sent to prison for the rest of your life. These are called consequences and life is littered with them.

There ARE situations and cultural norms' that demand you toe the line, unless anarchy is your thing, in which case, may I suggest therapy or counselling, you have to follow them and I am absolutely not advocating otherwise. There are written laws, obviously, but there is also an unwritten rules we adhere to as a societal collective. These laws and rules, by and large, are good. They are written and designed to keep up in socially acceptable check. They are not designed to remove our freedoms or ability to express ourselves independently. You can question the status quo, in many ways I actively encourage it, it's only through discussion and growth that we can encourage and enact social change. If we didn't do that, then workers would have no rights, women still wouldn't be able to vote, people within the L.G.B.T.Q.I.A+ community couldn't now be able to get married and people of colour would still be sat at the back of the bus. The people who helped mould society and the laws surrounding all of those changes, and many thousands like them, elicited change through the collective, through discussion and you may be one of these future people who help foster change for issues I don't even know about, and if you are, I implore you, continue to seek whatever truth you are searching for, but remain true to yourself and maybe, just maybe, by being a person pleaser, you might just, accidentally, end up being a people pleaser anyway, only this time in a good way.

I AM FUCKING EPIC

Never speak ill of yourself

This could be a direct follow up to don't be a people pleaser. This one is all about avoiding self deprecation. I self deprecate all the time, I mean ALL the time, but I do it to illicit a humorous response in any given situation, and to be clear, I'm not talking about this kind of behaviour. I'm talking about genuine self deprecation. I've already talked about neural pathways and how new synaptic pathways are formed and consolidated in as little as twelve weeks.

Imagine you've told yourself you are a piece of shit for twelve weeks, guess what? After twelve weeks, you're gonna believe you're a piece of shit. Now take your age, subtract five years for good measure, and imagine you've consistently told your self the same thing for that number of years. I'll take myself as an example. As stated, I'm 55 (at the time of writing this) now imagine if, every day of my life I'd told myself I was a piece of shit. I would have told myself 18, 250 times I was a piece of shit. Do you think I believe I'm a piece of shit? Too fuckin' right I do. I. AM. A. PIECE. OF. SHIT.

Now imagine I'd spent the last 50 years, 18,250 times, telling myself I was a worthy person, who deserves to achieve their goal(s). Do you think I'd be a different person? Absolutely I would, how could you not be. I guess what I'm trying to say in this section is, know your worth, or find your worth, whichever comes first and have the confidence to celebrate that worth, and if you've spent fifty years telling yourself you're a piece of shit, what do you do then? That, my friend, is the easy part, because as we've already established, it takes just twelve weeks to create an entirely new, stronger, pathway. You can literally think your way out of having a feeling of self worthlessness to a being a person who believes in their own self worth, and this isn't a diminished return over time.

You can do this today, you can do this over and over again, to cover any number of processes that trouble you. The trick? Well, there is no trick, but you DO have to commit. You have to believe, not necessarily in the final outcome, but you have to believe in the outcome. You have to commit to it, you can't be half assed. The problem is, of course, that at the beginning, you won't believe it. You've had years of conditioning to believe one thing and you're trying to rewire a program in your melon to say something completely different. You can do it and this is how you do it, and once you do it, you'll be amazed how easy it is and you'll do it over and over again. You get a small piece of paper or white card, I usually use a piece the size of a credit card and you write your affirmation on it. You write it down on that piece of paper and you put it in your wallet or your purse, and you take it out every day and you read it aloud. This helps de and re program your brain in so many ways. Firstly, you're not just thinking about something. Writing your affirmation down solidifies it. It makes an abstract and esoteric thought and manifest it into the world.

In essence, you've physically removed it from your head and created a real thing that you can read every day. It also forces you to consider what it is you want to change. You have to choose the words properly and writing them down helps to make sure that happens. It turns what you are thinking into a mantra you can utter every day and again, that stops your thought being some wishy-washy abstract thought, that can change and morph from day to day. The words are there, the thought process is there, the intent is there.

There is no ambiguity, you can read the actual words. This leads me on to the next part, what should you say and what should you not say? Well, the mantra is yours, but I would encourage you to not be ambiguous in your process. If you write "I will be a millionaire by the time I am 30" it's a little bit vague, don't you think? I mean it's fine, and you are allowed to believe it, but I'd be writing some other stuff on that card to consolidate that obscure statement.

"Every day I will make one connection to someone who can help me achieve my goal"

"I will enrol in night class and have my business degree in 4 years".

The ultimate point is that, in many ways, we reap what we sow. You say bad shit about yourself, you'll start believing that bad shit. You just will, it's how our brains work, they are hard wired to work like that, and there is nothing you can do about it. What you can do, is you can change it, you can choose HOW that hard wire process is developed. Confident, assured, forward thinking people don't always start out in life like that, they literally talk themselves into existence. You will become more confident if you tell yourself you are more confident. Our minds really are that strong and that amazing, but not as strong or amazing as you! See what I did there? She how I turned that around onto you? You can do that too. Do it as many times a day as you can, say it every single day, believe in your statements transformative ability and things will change, if change is something you're striving for. You might like you, you might not want to change you, you just want some positive affirmations. The changes you may want to illicit might be minor ones on a global scale. You might want to stop smoking, for example. The changes for you however will be life altering and, you know what, it's a thought process, you have nothing to lose by trying, and so much to gain when it works.

NB: If you smoke, STOP smoking! You've spending thousands of dollars a year on actively promoting your own death and/or years of miserable ill health by doing it. I recently discovered a pack of 50 cigarettes cost something like $75! Fucking $75, are you mental. I didn't put a question mark after that last sentence, I already know the answer. If you smoke 3 packs a week, that's almost @12,000.00 a year on smokes! Ten years of smoking-$120,000.00. It ages you before it kills you. It rots your teeth, makes your skin yellow, makes you stink - no, really! You absolutely stink the place out AND you are thousands of dollars out of pocket. I could devote an entire book on the side effects of smoking, but ultimately, stop doing it, you fucking idiot!

A DREAM IS WHERE A HOPE LIVES

Don't give up on your dreams

Dreams are, to a greater or lesser extent, what drives us as a race of creatures. You can have lofty dreams. I want to be the CEO of a Fortune 500 Company by the time I am 25. You can have modest dreams. I want to spend more quality time with my kids. You can disagree about dreams, the CEO could consider the family orientated dream a waste of time, the family orientated dreamer could consider the CEO foolish for not seeing their richest commodity, right in front of their eyes, family. Neither one is 'more' right than the other, they are equally right and equal important to the person who manifested them. Big or small, grand or personal, it really does not matter, what matters is you have something to believe in, strive for, a purpose. You remove that purpose and what do you become?

Dreamers rarely dream alone. Not in a collective sense anyway, but although that is a reality, there are exceptions to the rule. A football team can collectively dream of winning the World Cup for example, but what I mean here is that dreams are a moveable feast and never come as a single item. The person who dreams of becoming CEO at 25, what happens to them at 25 when they realise their ambition and become a CEO of a Fortune 500 Company at 25, do they stop dreaming? Of course they don't, they transplant the dream they have achieved for another one. The next one is usually slightly bigger and equally as hard to achieve and obtain than the dream they've just discarded and so it goes, one on top of the other, ad infinitum. Successful people can have several 'dreams' to achieve, in some discernible order.

Here's the thing, dreams change. You just have to remember to change with them. A kid dreams of being a spaceman (Space person!), is that dream achievable? Too fucking right it is! We can do almost anything we like, but that kid's dream might change the following year. Next year they might want to be a train driver, then the next year a vet, then the next year a... whatever! In the end Spaceman might literally be a million miles from where they started dreaming of their future, but if they manage to fulfil the dream they want to fulfil, then they have lived a blessed life. We are allowed to change, we are equally allowed to nail our feet to the floor, tell the world to go fuck itself and absolutely pursue the dream you've held onto since Kindergarten. A problem only manifests itself if our ability is not equal to our reach. If you are a grade C kid and to be an astronaut, you need to be an A+ student, all the rainbow unicorns in the world ain't gonna make you a fucking astronaut! BUT you could still go work for NASA or the space program somewhere. I need to be absolutely clear here, I'm not talking about abandoning your dreams, NO ONE has the right to take your dreams away from you, I just want you to manage your expectations. Brains, hard work, connections and a truck load of luck have a lot to do with how your life turns out. There are thousands of Oscar (tm) worthy actors out there who'll never get their break, should they stop acting? Of course not, but even acting which is, in many ways an organic art form, has skill attached to it. You don't go to drama school for three years for nothing. Acting is not easy, good acting is difficult, great acting is rare.

I don't care what your dream is. You might want to be the owner of your own company, an astronaut or an actor. The fact remains the same, irrespective of what you want to achieve-no one will fight harder for your dream than you! And if someone else is working harder than you, for you to achieve your goals, then those goals are not yours in the first place and you need to change your goals, and you need to have the courage to do that. Courage to pursue your goals or the courage to let them go. Blind faith in your ability is no faith at all, anymore than self praise is any kind of praise at all. If you're going to go for it, GO FOR IT! Don't pussyfoot around. Either take a shit, or get of the toilet! Give it every single thing you have because I promise you, when you are on your death bed, you won't be disappointed if you failed, you'll be disappointed if you did't try. If you tried and failed, you will still die a contented death. How about that for optimistic, hahaha.

IT'S GOOD TO LET ONE GO

Let go of what you can't control

Moaning! I cannot fucking stand it. It drives me insane. You know the type, people who look out a window and complain because it's raining - why? What's the fucking point? Complaining about the rain is not going to make it stop raining, nothing will. So buy a brolly, put a coat on, stay inside and stop fucking moaning. You moan because you're stuck in traffic, does the moaning make all the cars disappear? Of course it doesn't. You moan because you're stuck in a dead end job! No, no you're not. You're stuck because you're too chicken shit to change the job, unless you sold your soul to the packing factory and leaving would cost you your soul. Now don't be dumb about it, lock in another job before you give the one you hate the flick, but you are not 'stuck' in a job. You're not 'stuck' in a loveless marriage. You choose to stay, consciously or subconsciously, because staying is ironically easier than trying to leave. Leaving will, probably, be temporarily uncomfortable, but would you rather six months of misery, or thirty years? If it's not working for you, do something about it.

Don't be 'that person' at the office who spends all day talking about how fucking useless their partner is and how you'd be a million times better off if you just walked away. A million times better, really? A million? You'd be a MILLION times better off if you left and you still haven't left! You wouldn't see me for dust. I would be gone, because who doesn't want to be a million times better off? Now you might want to talk it through, you might want to try couples counselling, a trial separation, something. I'm not suggesting you just walk around muttering 'fuck it' under your breath, while you casually burn every bridge you ever built down to the ground, but if you've tried, like really tried, and you know it ain't gonna work no more, that's when it's time to pick up sticks and walk away.

Thing is, we all know when that is. We might not want to recognise it, but we do. Have you ever been dumped? Or dumped someone? Ever try to hold on to a love you knew, with all your heart, was no longer there? Do you remember just how fucking brutal and useless that was? When it's gone baby, it's gone! That's when you have to let go, because it's no longer in your control. There is real calm in the eye of a storm, a stillness you won't find anywhere else in the world. There is an unruffled tranquility to that inevitability. If you can't stop death, why worry about dying? Why not put all that energy into actually living? Into being fearless and being honest.

Tell that girl, or guy you fancy, that you fancy them, what's the outcome going to be? They either say they don't feel the same and you're embarrassed for like two minutes, or you have the best root of your life, you fall in love and live happily ever after! Isn't the risk of that worth a chance of discomfort? Fear can stop you from doing any number of things, but own that fear, grab it by the neck and ride that bitch into the ground and you are unstoppable. Be aware of the little things, but don't let them control you. Weather, traffic, queues at the shops, you shouldn't be giving any one of those things to change how you feel or think or behave. Stuck in traffic? Find an alternative route. Can't find an alternative route? Then there's no getting around the fact you're stuck in traffic. Listen to some music or do what I do and listen to a book. I have exponentially increased my knowledge of-Alfred Hitchcock, the works of Friedrich Nietzsche, Carl Gustav Jung, the bible, investing, a brief history of time, Greek Gods and Monsters and the complete works of Sir Arthur Conan Doyle, William Shakespeare, Oscar Wild and Jane Austin, to name but a few. All from the comfort of my car. Do you think I have a negative mindset when it comes to traffic? If it rains, I'm out in it. I sing "Singin' in the Rain" and splash in puddles, I don't even put the hood up on my coat! Do I care if it's raining? Rain gives me the chance to sing, why would I not like rain?

When I was young, when I had my first bedsit, the one I've mentioned already. I had very little money. I would go to the market and buy a tray of broken eggs. They were not broken, but they were seconds and I got a tray of 24 for a few dollars. I'd buy a big bag of spuds and 14 Tins of home brand baked beans and a packet chocolate cake mix (because I already had the eggs) I'd bake a cake and carefully slice that cake into 14 pieces. I'd then carefully wrap those 14 pieces of cake into individual freezer bags and freeze them. I knew, for around $20 a fortnight, I'd have a big plate of fried eggs, chips and beans for my dinner AND a slice of chocolate cake (and a cup of tea) for afters. I never got a taxi, I rarely got the bus, I walked everywhere. Subsequently I was super fit and super thin. Did I care I had no money? Hell no, it was a blessing, besides which, I couldn't change anything there and then, so I didn't sweat it. I was putting myself through college at the time and eventually I got a part time job, money was better and I knew I could survive pretty much anything I was faced with.

If you can change something, or your part within it, then do that. Worry about global warming, child poverty and big businesses avoiding taxes.

Don't worry about the weather, getting rejected from someone you fancy or any of the small stuff, it really doesn't matter.

I don't know if this next 'bit' fits into this category or not, but I'll wedge it in anyway because its about letting go of what you can't control and I think it's so incredibly important. I just want to touch on sexuality, sexual orientation and gender identity. I'm 55, I don't know all the right terms, fuck I have difficulty trying to remember the pronouns, but I am trying, I promise. The thing is, it doesn't matter if it's your brother, your cousin, your son, daughter or sister. Hell it could be your Mom or Dad. If someone you love identifies as a member of the LGTBQIA+ community-for the love of fucking God, just accept them! They are more together and have more courage than you could ever comprehend. Imagine the guts it takes to:
1. Come to the realisation that they belong to which ever part of that community they belong, and,
1. Stand in front of you and actually tell you.

I cannot imagine the amount of courage it would take to have that conversation with a parent, for example. To emotionally expose yourself to someone, to the extent that you think you might lose that persons love forever! FUCK that's unimaginably difficult, and yet thousands of kids do it every day and every day hundreds of kids are abandoned by the very people who should be there to protect them and love them unconditionally. That's what unconditionally means, If you're one of those, shame on you.

As someone who's a boring cis white, heterosexual male, I don't have all the answers, I'm not even sure I know most of the questions. I had to actually Google LGTBQIA+ because I wasn't sure about all the letters. It was only ever gay and lesbian in my day (roll eyes emoji) What I do know, is that discrimination, homophobia, bigotry and hate have no place in a modern society, so just let go of it. My eldest daughter asked me, the other week, what I'd do if she was gay? I said I wouldn't 'do' anything. I'd still love her, accept her and worry for her future, just like I always will. I'd just hope whoever she met treated her with the loving respect she deserved. She said she wasn't gay, but wanted to know what I thought. I think I passed that one.

I will say, and I'm sure I'll get letters for this, I have to say one thing. The LGTBQI+ community often say they feel like outsiders and not accepted. I humbly request that the acronym contain the letter H for heterosexual, because I believe you can't belong to the larger community if you still identify and belong to a smaller one. Let's just be ONE community. It's like hating someone because they are tall or have blonde hair or are left handed! It just doesn't make any sense. Equally, I don't care what religion you follow, or don't follow. I don't care about the colour of your skin, other than I care that it bothers other people-fucking pricks! Any more than I care what shoe size you are. I care if I'm at the gym and I'm stood next to you in the showers and you've got a massive cock and you make me feel like I've got a dick like a baby acorn in comparison, I fucking care then! But mostly, I just care about whether you are good people, oh, and if you tried to touch my noodle in said shower, I'd really be quite bothered then. I'm a good 75%-85% sure I'd tell you to stop, okay, probably about 67%.

Be good people and let go of all that bullshit you can't change anyway, just let go of what you can't control and I assure you, you'll be happier, and freer, for it.

MAIN PLAYERS TO SET

Stay clear of the drama

Do you have a friend, relative or co-worker who always seems to be in the thick of some kind of life changing drama? Me too, ain't they just the most annoying pricks in the world!

I'll tell you something about those people. Sure, some of them suffer their own micro dramas, and those dramas are real, but most only have drama in the first place because they won't keep their fucking noses out of other peoples business.

Oscar Wilde once said "There's only one thing worse than being talked about, and that's not being talked about"

That's some funny and witty shit right there, but I humbly suggest Oscar, that you are talking out of your arse! I don't know anyone who 'likes' being talked about, not one and some of these people suffer drama, despite trying everything to avoid it.

"So Steve said to Carol that he'd seen Geoff with Alison, down the cinema last week, and Geoff was holding hands with Alison and they both appeared very friendly, if you know what I mean. Then Geoff saw Steve and Geoff was all like, hey Steve, just dropping Alison off, to meet her boyfriend, and Geoff doesn't even drive 'cos he got banned for drink driving two months ago, but he doesn't know I know that, so don't tell him. Besides Alison doesn't even have a boyfriend and Geoff had his own popcorn and Alison was bright red, like, get me the fuck out of here red! Anyway, besides...... "

And on and on and on they go, sucking all the oxygen out of the room and slowly making you wish you were dead! You get two of these word vampires in a room together and all hope is lost. The thing is, for the most part, they're just harmless people, trying to fill the void of silence* Or, if they are stuck with their own thoughts, they might not actually like what they're thinking, so they block it out with endless noise. They could, equally, just be the fun loving, go-getting, life and soul of the party. They type of person everyone tends to gravitate to, naturally, effortlessly.

If they are the former, and not the latter, you want to try and avoid them! Run, run away, hide in the hills. Change your name and grow a beard. Seriously, even if you're a woman, grow a beard! I don't use this word often, and when I do, it's usually just for dramatic effect, but I do believe these types of people are toxic and it doesn't matter if it's consciously, subconsciously, intended or unintended. These people will do you harm, if it's easier, instead of asking yourself "How do I get rid of these toxic people?" Ask yourself "Why are these people in my life, why do I give them significance?".

Over in the UK, many years ago, there was a woman at work, I could not stand her, don't worry, she despised me almost as much as I disliked her. She wasn't a 'bad' person, in fact in many ways she was.... Okay, but we did NOT get on. We didn't like each other and we barely tolerated each other. We disliked each other so much, in fact, that should she ever read this, without ever mentioning her name, she'd know exactly who it was I was talking about, and so would everyone else. To many people she was just a little... brisk. A little abrasive, sharp even. I saw her as toxic. Not happy unless she was moaning and complaining, or belittling someone, or asserting her superiority. Mean enough to get you upset, not mean enough to end up in HR, you know the type. Thing is, I know the type too, and I gave her absolutely NO power over me whatsoever, and I think that's one of the reasons she disliked me so much. I wouldn't play into her game, I wouldn't give her the fuel she needed to fan the flames of her power play and like a vine that withers and dies, if you don't water it, hate and toxicity are the same. It's like putting a lit candle in a bell jar, the lack of oxygen snuffs out the flame. I encourage every single one of you to snuff out those flames. The fumes coming off those flames are toxic, deprive them of their means of existing and your life will be better for it.

How do you remove these cancerous people from your life? Well, in some instances, you just can't. You might work with them, they might be family, or extended family. So it's not always about cutting the cancer out. You can't just tell Aunty Jean to go fuck off, can you? Why not? If enough people told Aunty Jean to fuck off, Aunty Jean might end up actually questioning her behaviour and if she doesn't, well at least you've told her to fuck off and she's no longer your problem. Toxic people do not like honest people and they really don't like honest people who stand their ground, and Aunty Jean might just have to find herself accountable for her own actions/words. If you really can't tell Jean to take a long walk off a tall cliff, then the next best thing is to avoid where possible, just limit the amount of exposure you have to them, or they have to you. They WILL get the message, and if they ask you why you're avoiding them, well, they asked you to explain yourself, it wasn't you. Now you can tell her to fuck off, and you can tell her why she needs to fuck off.

That doesn't always work mind.

The flip side of people who 'create' drama, of course, are those who crave it and if the opportunity presents itself, they can create a destructive, or indestructible (depending on what side of the drama you're living on) perfect little drama, every single time you meet. You got that one friend who always has shit happen 'to' them? The shit magnet? Consciously or subconsciously, these people are your King or Queen of drama. I was trying to think of an example and I thought about domestic violence. Now, please don't reach for the pitch forks and burn me at the steak. I'm NOT talking about an abusive relationship like, traditionally, a man beats his wife because, I don't know, she took twenty-seconds longer to make his morning coffee, or some shit like that and clearly she deserved it, because otherwise, why would she be late with his coffee? That shit is fucked up and if a 'man' hits a woman, then I hope she gets to stick a bread knife in his chest and I hope she gets arrested and found not guilty and set free, all on the same day and she moves on with her life and gets to live the one she wants it to be.

Just to contextualise that: **1 in 6** (17%) women and 1 in 16 (6.1%) men have experienced physical and/or sexual violence from a current or ex-partner. 1 in 4 (23%) women and 1 in 6 (16%) men have experienced emotional abuse from a current or ex-partner. 1 in 5 (18%) women and 1 in 20 (4.7%) men have experienced sexual violence.

If you're a man reading this and you really want to know how not to be a dick, then just stop thinking with your dick and your fists and discharge your patriarchal egos. Women can be abusive too, of course they can, the stats clearly identify that, but they are nowhere near as fucking evil as men.

No, I'm talking the Richard Burton/Liz Taylor kind of abusive relationship. She gave as good as he did, he'd slap her, she'd try and scratch his eyes out, or visa versa. I don't actually know if their relationship was physically abusive like that, but I do know it was volatile and I know it wasn't all one sided, they were pretty evenly matched. They loved each other and hated each other in equal measure and a relationship like that was never going to be anything other than high maintenance and none sustainable. Each one created the drama and each one craved it. Most Richards find their Liz's and most Liz's find their Richards, and in situations like that, you can't stay away from the drama, you strive for it.

If you can avoid drama, then avoid it, or those who create it AND if you want to be clear of it, then do so in small incremental steps. You don't have to make wide sweeping gestures or statements, just small changes. Richard and Liz fought like cat and dog, but ultimately, they still respected each other and, for a time, their relationship. They were symbiotic, most abusive relationships are not that lucky. Get out any way you can. Go to the police, the council, a shelter, your family, a friend, a co-worker, just run away and never look back.

I went from avoiding drama to domestic abuse real quickly there didn't I! Makes you wonder if I was ever the victim of domestic abuse? Well, I did get slapped once, but the girl was pretty and we had a pre-arranged safety word! (Tangerine) I had an abusive step father, if I need to be honest. My mother knew, no one else did. He'd beat me often enough. Broke three teeth out of my head with a single punch once. How did I escape? I ran away and lived on the streets for six months, then I got my shit together. So yeah, I know about domestic violence. I know it's painful, I know you feel like you have nowhere to go, and you'll suffocate under the pressure. I know it feels like you have no one to turn to, no one to talk to, no one to ask, beg, scream for help, but I also know there is hope, light, help, breathing space. If you're in an abusive relationship, and that doesn't always mean partner, it could be parent or child or sibling, friend, co-worker or extended member of your family. I can be anyone. I can promise you this, if you take that first step, there will be someone out there to help you take that journey. You will feel alone, but you are not. You are not alone, you are worthy of help, you deserve it, but you gotta take that first step.

You think about that level of trauma, then consider Dave the dick at work who always steals your yogurt, you can handle Dave and the drama he creates. Personally, I'd get some liquid laxatives, inject about four doses into a yogurt and wait for the son-of-a-bitch to steal it. I bet he wouldn't do it again lol.

Drama is like a puddle in the Street. Most of the time, they are avoidable. You can navigate around them and move on. Sometimes though, you just have to jump in, feet first, wade through it and get to the other side whilst staying as dry as possible. You can't control the weather, you can't control where the puddles will manifest themselves, you can't control how big or how deep they are, but you can decide if you're going to try and avoid them, or are you gonna splash around a bit, to get through it? There is nothing boring or vanilla or safe about avoiding drama. Avoiding drama is great, you just have to recognise it for what it is and move away from it, wherever possible, unless you actively seek out high drama, if you're a Formula One racing driver for example. I suspect that life to be quite drama filled, and that's okay or if you're the 'Ace' reporter and the editor is holding the front page for you, or you work in the Armed Forces, or the

Police, or you're a Paramedics. In real terms, I guess what I need to be saying is, if drama is too much for you, then avoid it. Something, anything, only needs to be avoided if it does you harm, has the potential to do you harm or you even perceive it as being potentially harmful, that's when you have to step away. Just do what feels right for you and you won't go too far wrong, assuming of course that your normal is normal!

Good luck.

* NB The void of silence does not need to be filled. Sometimes the void just likes being the void. Those with kids will understand this more than those that don't.

IT'S ALL YOU NEED

Love
noun
noun: love; plural noun: loves
1. An intense feeling of deep affection
verb
Verb: love; 3rd person present: loves; past tense: loved; past participle: loved; gerund or present participle: loving.
"Nothing you can make that can be made
No one who can save that can't be saved
Nothing you can do
But can learn to be you in time
It's easy
All You Need Is Love'

Songwriters: Paul McCartney / John Lennon
The Beatles

Love is all you need! Is that true? Does that even make sense? No, of course it doesn't. It's just an incredibly catchy pop song from 1967. If your car broke down on the freeway, love isn't going to fix it, you're going to need a mechanic. Love doesn't come with a 1/8 torque wrench. Well, it might, but I think you'd have to ring a very specific number to obtain that kind of service! There are, as we all know, many different types of love, on many different levels. I'm sure, for example, that you love your second cousin, on your mothers side, but do you love them as much as you love your sister, or brother or your dad? You might, but it's rare, to find someone who loves you so unconditionally. The trouble with 'love' is that we use the term SO much now, it's almost lost its meaning. We love a TV show, a movie star, a book, a painting, an item of clothes, our favourite cup for tea, our favourite cup for coffee, a pillow, a parking spot! A fucking parking spot? We can like all that shit. We can like it till the cows come home, but do we really love that stuff? Would you die for Schitt's Creek or Game of Thrones? Or would you jump in front of a bus for them, or would you jump in front of a bus to save your child's life?

*I mean an actual, moving bus, not one that's like parked up… Just to be clear.

So, there are, as far as I can make sense, two types of love. Two and only two: Internal and external. External love is something we project. It's this love that loves Schitt's Creek and Game of Thrones, or that shirt, or those shoes you wear, or that album you listened to last week. Sure, you still have to be the one feeling it, but it is external love that is projected inwards. Now don't get me wrong, I love LOTS of things. I love spicy food and Audrey Hepburn. I love Superman: The Movie, still the best movie ever made, but I love Raiders of the Lost Ark, Blade Runner and Casino Royale too. I love The Six Million Dollar Man, Voyage to the Bottom of the Sea and Buffy the Vampire Slayer. I love Dean Martin and Doris Day. I love the collective works of Paulo Coelho, Shakespeare, Oscar Wilde and Daniel Defoe's Robinson Crusoe, the colour blue and my mustard yellow Vans, a walk on the beach on a clear and cold autumn day and that worldly stillness just before sunrise. I love a lot of things. I am a man made of Lego (tm) man, and every brick is made up of something I love, BUT those things, every single one of them, they are still external 'loves' projected inwards. Sure I had to internally process how I felt about all of them and then assign a feeling towards them, but we do that all the time, on a subconscious level, so that 'love' does come from me, but it's a superficial love. I've not internalised it, I've not allowed it in and made it part of my DNA. I loved The Man From U.N.C.L.E, so much so that I desperately wanted to dye my hair blonde and be called Illya. I'm Irish, with jet black hair, do you have any idea what happens to jet black hair when you try to dye it with a hair dye from the local chemist? I'll tell you, it makes your hair go a shimmering, shiny copper gold. You could have seen my head from space, it was that bright and shiny-fucking idiot I was. Anyway, I digress. I loved The Man From U.N.C.L.E, and when it got cancelled, after three brilliantly blissful seasons, I was gutted, but I moved on. I got over it. I adopted a 'oh well' approach to it, after all, what else could I do? I didn't crumble into dust and get blown away by tears. I just got over it and that's because, although the love for that show came from me, I didn't give it any truly emotional weight, I didn't allow my external love for something to penetrate through to my internal love process. It's that level of love that gets you hurt. External love is the hard, husky shell, internal love is the soft, mushy nut it protects. It's important that you use and exercise both.

Internal love, that's for family (hopefully) a few friends, your partner and, if you have then, your kids. Internal love is the stuff you'd kill for, and more importantly, die for. Anyone tries to hurt my kids, I'm going to hurt them. I'll die an old man in prison, or a young one walking to the gas chamber, a content man, knowing I protected my girls (Well, that got dark real quick! Let's flip that).

Point is, both serve a purpose, both deserve to be aa part of us and both help us become or remain, a strong, rounded and grounded human being. Learn to love, to embrace the passion. Stoke those internal fires and have the heat rage out of you. Love a movie or a book or shirt, but also love family, friends, what you do for a living and who you do it with. Uncontrolled passion can turn into ugly obsession, we don't want that. We want you to be able to walk through life confident, strong and caring. You need to know you can love and be loved and whilst that makes you vulnerable, ironically, it actually makes you stronger and damn it, it just makes you feel better.

To love anything, externally or internally is scary. It makes you vulnerable. Loving a book isn't scary, I hear you shout into these pages, well try posting you like something on social media and see how many new arse holes you get ripped, but you are right, those external loves do not penetrate deep. You won't expose your vulnerability much by liking a 'thing'. Internal love however, that's an entirely different barrel of cats!

Internal love. The deep, penetrating love that scars and lasts a lifetime, that's different, you mine a little deeper and strike a vein of love, you've hit gold and the pain you might feel is worth it because of the joy you do feel. I don't want this to turn into a soppy, mush-fest, but I know you know what I mean. Well, I hope you know what I mean. We don't always have family or friends, some of us are lonely and alone, even some people who are surrounded by many others. If you've got no one, and it's practical to do so, get a dog, or a cat, or a parrot! It's important to know you CAN love and it's all right to do so. Sometimes you'll feel vulnerable and exposed, but it really is worth it. Love people and things all you like. Open up your heart and let that stuff pour in, and out! You will feel joyful and connected and it's quite obvious, hopefully, that a life filled with love is way better than a life filled with hate, or worse, a like filled with a blank, nothingness void.

Smile, connect, say good morning to people, hold the door open for someone, offer to help or listen. We all have the ability to do better than we do, especially in these trying and troubling times (Covid 19, war, famine, poverty, and a world filled with bitterness and hate). We all need to know we are loved, we have a voice, we are listened to and someone does care, and we are allowed to care back, it doesn't make us weak, it shows everyone, including ourselves, that we are strong enough to love and care, and that's a powerful statement right there. Embrace that, hold on to that, nurture that, encourage it to grow, and you will grow with it. Just breath and love.

The greatest thing
    You'll ever learn
    Is just to love
    And be loved
    In return

    Moulin Rouge (2001)
    Sung by David Bowie
    Song Writer: Eden Ahbez

BE GOOFY

Adjective INFORMAL

adjective: goofy; comparative adjective: goofier; superlative adjective: goofiest

1. NORTH AMERICAN

   foolish or harmlessly eccentric

Hello spunk knuckles! How's your day been? Are you reading this in the morning, over a coffee, are you reading it at night, snuggled up in a nice, cosy bed, or are you listening to it in the car on the way to work? I hope it's not the latter, otherwise you'll have to listen to me prattle on in my, not so broad, Mancunian accent telling you to be goofy.

And why the hell would I be doing that? Well, since you asked so nicely, I guess I have to tell you.

My eldest sister is around ten years older than me, the point of me telling you this is, if you actually met my sister, like sat down and had a chat, you'd think she was 25! (Internally that is. Externally she's all but completely haggard and worn out) She's maintained her youthful interior because out of everyone I know or anyone I've ever known, she is the most joyful person I've ever met! She oozes joy from every pore of her body and if you are lucky enough to get stuck in a room with her, she'll have you laughing your ass off in about 5 minutes flat.

As with everything, there are several types of joy. The joy you feel when you get married, for example, is different to the joy you feel when your first child is born. Whatever triggers your joy, one thing remains constant-you. You are your own Northern Star, you are the Captain of your own ship and you can sail it in any direction you see fucking fit! You want to be a beige clothes wearing miserable twat, riding around on public transport, smelling of piss and complaining about everything in the world, from the kids today to your haemorrhoids, that's your choice. Yes, life can be shitty and it can sometimes work really hard to fuck you up and, ironically, drag you down, but life can kiss my big, hairy balls if it thinks it's going to get the better of me. Whenever I go shopping, I say the same thing: "I'm going to the shops to get stuff I don't need, with money I don't have" and anti-joy, the stuff that drags you down, makes you sad, that's the same stuff. It's just stuff, things. Yes, you might be stuck with an electric bill and you don't know how you're going to pay it, but there is an answer, telephone the electricity company and have a chat with them. Tell them you're struggling and need some help or time or support and most of the time, they'll be cool about it.

Don't let 'stuff' dictate how you feel. Stuff will come and stuff will go, but you will remain the constant. So, with that in mind, how the hell do you become joyful? Well, there are lots of ways, obviously, and this is not a comprehensive list, but:

Stop waiting to be happy. Happy is as happy does. Subconsciously stuff can get us down, but if we make a conscientious effort to work against that, if we choose to be happy, something quite magical happens-we become happier. You just have to recognise the opportunities when they present themselves. Opportunities come and go into our lives all the live long day. Someone serves you coffee, smile, say thanks and make eye contact. I promise, you'll both feel awesome when you do. It's about changing your perspective slightly and why not? If you're not happy, then something isn't fucking working. What you have is broken, so it's time to swap things up.

Add happiness, like seasoning to food, to your life. I get it, overworked and under paid, general money worries, Covid, kids, the car has a slow flat, your food is cold, your beer is warm. The heating system in your house just blew up and you're getting too fat, even for your 'fat' jeans. Life can well and truly suck and finding one chink of joy in this joyless mother fucking life can, sometimes, be hard, BUT there is joy there, I promise you. Even if it's in the dumbest fucking thing, like the beauty of a flower (Puke!), but it is true. Sometimes however, you have to inject your own joy and that's a snake eating its own tail kind of story, if ever I heard one. In order to become joyful, you have to inject joy into your own life, but if your life is joyless, how the hell do you do that? It's like when these people in the internet say the best way to become rich is to invest $1000 a month in a wide range of stocks and shares! Dude, if I had $100 spare a month, I think I'd be rich enough not to worry about being rich. The main difference, of course, is that joy isn't tangible, it's ethereal, it's a thought, it's not tangible like a case full of cash is. Well, I hear you say, if I had any fucking joy in my life, I'd be joyful already right! Well, no, not necessarily. Think of joy like music. You don't walk around all day with music bouncing around your brain, even in musicals, people stop singing and talk once in a while. Your head is not stuffed to bursting with music, but if you want to sing a song, you start singing. Joy is like that. Yes, it's harder to obtain, you have to mine your thoughts a little deeper, but it's there, like the song you haven't sung yet.

Make self-care part of your daily routine. Self-care, self-care, self-care! What new age bullshit am I trying to sell to you now? Well, there's the obvious; brush your teeth, take a shower, eat well and remain hydrated. Take some physical exercise and try to talk to at least one person a day, other than yourself in the mirror, but there's the mental stuff too, do a jigsaw puzzle, or a crossword or (my favourite) play online backgammon. I'm now quietly confident in my ability to whip someone's ass in backgammon! Read a book, meditate, you can even Netflix and chill, but you have to put in a little work first. Firstly, get your house in order, literally! I mean tidy up, empty the bins, put the laundry away, prep dinner, that kind of stuff. You can't truly relax if you know you've got twenty things to do after you've snapped out of your relaxed mode, because guess what? You won't really reach relax mode. That'll piss you off, that pissed off mood will stress you out even more and welcome to the cause and effect loop.

Write a bucket list. I mean, don't be a dick about it. If your bucket list reads like this:
    i. Become a millionaire
    ii. Bang that 20 year old with the big tits from that shop I went in yesterday.
    (I don't think I can even begin to dissect how much of that sentence is just wrong)
    iii. Buy a Ski-jet (Wanker!)
Then, already, I know you're a fucking tool and I probably want nothing to do with you, I mean, apart from other jet-ski owners, who'd want to hang around with you?

But if your bucket list is:
    i. Finish my education
    ii. Run a marathon
    iii. Tidy up

    iv. Climb the Sydney Harbour Bridge
    v. Work on my manners, say please and thank you more

Then I think I could spend some time with you. I think I would enjoy your company and have a great time, and probably want to do it some more. The bucket list doesn't have to be massive, either in scope or length or task, it just has to be yours and when you tick something off that list, even if it's just 'doing the dishes' guess what? You feel better, because you've accomplished something. Well, you did two things. You accomplished your task and you actively worked towards bringing joy into your life-boom! Well done.

3. Laugh. "Sometimes I have to think really hard to remember the last time I laughed" is not something you want to find yourself saying too often. I laugh a lot, several times a day in fact. I fine humour in the most mundane of situations and everything can be reduced to a punch-line. Laughing reduces stress, improves blood flow, boosts our immunity and damn it, makes you feel better! I have my 'go to' places for instant laughter and joy. Any scene from The Morecambe and Wise Show, or Peter Sellers in any Pink Panther movie, Ronnie Barker in Porridge or any episode of Only Fools and Horse for a starter, the other night however, it was my wife who had me in a virtual state of apoplexy. It was the kind of laughter that hurts your throat and stops you from breathing. The more I laughed, the more she laughed, the more she laughed, the more I laughed and on and on it went, until we were useless to each other. It was a joyous moment and one of the many reasons I love her so much.

4. Surround yourself with happy people. Well, duh! If I could avoid dickheads, how fucking better would my life be? Don't answer that, it's a rhetorical question. You can't surround yourself with happy people. You might be stuck with Derek from maintenance, and he's a completely humourless twat! Derek might even know he's a twat and not actually give a toss. You might work with Derek and although he is completely joyless and you can't avoid him completely, you don't have to spend your free time with Derek, you can spend your free time with Alan, Alan is ace. He's funny, bright and definitely knows how to make you laugh. Alan is joy!

Be like Alan.

YOU CAN RING MY BELL

Telephone your mother.

Look, I get that some of you probably don't have a mother. Perhaps you never did or, like me, you might have moved away when you was young and lost that connection, or never really connected in the same way. I had a very turbulent relationship with my mother and I'm gonna spend a shit load of money on therapy, in the hope of one day understanding our relationship, but what I do know, is that she died in December 2020 in the UK and covid stopped me from going over to England and paying my last respects. My mother is gone, she ain't never coming back and I'll never get the chance to say hi, tell her I love her, or give her a hug and even though we never saw eye to eye, if I could, I'd still ring her and tell her I loved her. If yours is still around, go fuckin' tell her, or tell your dad or your brother, or your cousin, or whoever, because forever is a fucking long time!

"Ring your mum" really, is about holding on and maintaining a relationship that is, or should be, significant. Build bridges, build them before they fall down. Make them strong, durable and impenetrable.

Get a chance to go around to your sisters for Sunday lunch, take it. Got the opportunity to take your Pop down the RSL for a pint Saturday afternoon, do it. Your brother asks you to join him to watch him play in his local soccer team, just do it. Every yes or no situation is a moment lost, or a memory gained. We only have a finite number of grains of sand in out hour glass, spend them wisely. Make sure every grain is accounted for, and that doesn't mean binge watching nine seasons of your favourite show. It's about getting out there, connecting, doing something. Switch the TV off, switch the phone and either connect or re-connect.

I love my phone, I do. It's like a mini office in my pocket and I use it all the time, but it's a bugbear of mine that it would appear that whilst phones are getting smarter, the people operating them are getting dumber. A recent study showed that whilst social media exposure, globally, is growing and our 'connections and likes' are even higher, most people are feeling more socially distant and anxious than ever. Some of that was to do with covid, but most was due to the disconnect between the reality of who a person is and who they project themselves to be on social media. We've all done it, filters, backgrounds, stamps, lighting. Made ourselves look younger, thinner, brighter eyed and more 'interesting'. When in reality, we are just 'normal' but now, normal isn't good enough, normal is boring and old and lame. Some people won't even go out of their houses anymore because the reality of who they are doesn't match the projection of who they are on social media.

You know who don't care what filter you use on social media? Your mum (hopefully) and if it's not your mum, then whoever you consider significant in your life: Dad, best friend, sister. You NEED someone in your life who's prepared to tell you your pimple is massive, or you've got spinach in your teeth, or the shoes you're wearing are hideous. You can't airbrush your life away. You have to maintain those relationships, especially now, whilst we are significantly socially disadvantaged and that takes work. Hard work and often, like, oh I don't know, ringing your mum!

WHO DOESN'T LIKE A PAGE TURNER?

Read a book or two

I read, on average, a book a week. I aim for two, but I really don't have the time (Or the eyesight) to read more and I tend to listen to books whilst I'm driving. It's easy and convenient. It also means I'm not clogging up my house with books and, it has to be said, for the times in which this book is being written, I can't physically go out and buy books anyway. I can order on line, but that's when I tend to know what I want, not a browsing type situation.

There are more important things in this world than how I order my books however, and I think it's more important to focus on the facts I'm ordering the books in the first place. I rarely read fiction books, as a writer, I don't like to pollute my brain with other peoples ideas, it clouds my own creative process, but I love and adore biographies and books that expand my knowledge. I loved Seth Rogen's Yearbook, one of the few books that have made me actually laugh out loud, Matthew McConaughey's Greenlight and Mythos and Heroes, both by Stephen Fry.

So WHY should you read more? Well, why not is my first answer, but then, if you do a Google search of benefits of reading, you'll get the following:

1. Improves brain connectivity. It used to be said that you need to exercise your brain, just like any other muscle, but it turns out the brain isn't a muscle after all, it's an organ (snigger). True it's an organ that helps control all your muscles, but it one itself. It's a great big, fat, grey organ! That being said, using it still has massive benefits and although it's not a muscle, the old saying of you don't use it, you loose it certainly applies and it has been proven time and time again that using your brain, actively using your brain can prevent cognitive decline in the aged.
2. It increases your vocabulary and comprehension. That just goes without saying, right? The more words you are exposed to and the more you comprehend them, the greater your vocabulary. You read your books as kids, when you knew no words, and then, as if by magic, you started to know more words, then more, and more. Soon, you were stringing together a few words, then sentences and finally, you could have full blown sentences!

3. Reading before bed aids sleep. We all know that right? I can be in bed, thrashing around like a cat in a pillow case, chasing sleep that's coming nowhere near me and I open a book and I'm like five sentences in and I'm out for the count. I think it might have something to do with over working tired eyes, also, if reading is part of a healthy sleep hygiene program, you're self triggering the sleep hormones and telling your brain it's time to sleep and, of course, reading helps to lower blood pressure and heart rates, which also aid good sleep.
4. Reading goes hand in hand with writing, right? You a good reader, you're eventually gonna become a good writer. You read good books, you get to understand cadence, fluidity, structure, tone, pacing and all the other influencing elements, that go into great writing.

And
5. Stronger analytical thinking skills. Ever read Agatha Christie or Steven King or Doyles's Sherlock Holmes and figures out who did the crime before you got to the end of the book? Ta-dar! You're a great analytical thinker and chances are, that all started many years ago, when you picked up your first book, with your grubby, sticky lolly hands and began to read. To be fair, that sounds like me most Saturday nights 'cos it's a 'cheats' night, but you get the idea.
6. Reading is sexy. No, it's not! Yes, it is! There is a whole sub culture of sexy geeks and nerds! You read a book, or read a book whilst wearing a pair of glasses and well… we've all seen the movie, right?

NIGHT, NIGHT, SLEEP TIGHT

Get a good nights sleep

Oh my GOD! I wish someone had exalted nugget of pure gold to me many, many years ago. Firstly, let me say this-I am a writer. I write at night and work all day. I am genetically encoded to have shite sleep. I am also a classic Owl, my poor, long suffering wife is a Lark, but not to worry, we work things out. Add to that, I am a clinically diagnosed insomniac and sleep, or the lack there of, is something I am a fucking expert on!

So people, like me, once they get to bed, sleep like a baby. Now I have been known to go a while on only three and a half hours a sleep a night, that's pretty rough, but, I have to say, they are a pretty good three and a half hours. It never used to be a problem, until I hit the big 4-0 and my metabolism suddenly told me to go fuck myself, then the kilos started to creep on, just one at first, then three, then five, then I turn around, I'm fifty-five and look like the Goodyear blimp! Obesity is insidious, it crawls into your life ounce by ounce and we are all, strongly, blinded to it, until it's too late, but guess what! It's not too late. You can do something about it and the first thing you can do about it is sort your sleep out.

So, let's hit you with the bad news first, and holy hell, is there a LOT of bad news! I tell you what, I'll ease you in slowly, so not to scare or scar you. I'll just concentrate on one organ, for now. Let's take The Heart! Some of the most serious problems associated with a lack of sleep include High blood pressure, heart attack, heart failure and stroke! Hows that for a starter? Tell you what, let's add increased risk of dementia, diabetes, obesity, depression and low sex drive. You want more? You got it. Your immune system in severely compromised. You'll be cranky, irritable and you more than likely, look like shit warmed up. A lack of sleep could, quite literally, fucking kill you!

In a couple of pages I'm going to give you the tools to improve your irregular sleep. The tools I am about to give you might even fix the problem full stop, but you firstly, have to recognise there is a problem and secondly, want to do something about it!

But first...

There are many reasons why you can't sleep and yes, I've actually done some real, honest to God research on it. According to a paper published 19 May 2017 called:

Short- and long-term health consequences of sleep disruption

Goran Medic,1,2 Micheline Wille,1 and Michiel EH Hemels1

The authors wrote:
Risk factors contributing to sleep deprivation and disruption

Category	Risk factors
Lifestyle	• Consuming excessive amounts of caffeine
	• Drinking alcohol
	• Drug abuse
	• Shift work
	• Attending university
	• Jet lag
Environmental	• Excessive noise, such as industrial wind turbines
	• Excessive light
Psychosocial	• Anxiety, worry, and rumination
	• Parents of young children
	• Caregivers to a family member with a chronic, life-threatening, or terminal illness
Sleep disorder	• Insomnia
	• Obstructive sleep apnea
	• Restless leg syndrome
	• Narcolepsy
	• Circadian rhythm disorders
Medical conditions	• Pain
	• Restrictive lung disease
	• Chronic kidney disease
	• Diabetes
	• Neurodegenerative diseases
	• Psychiatric disorders
	• Use of certain medications

Did someone say fuck me sideways with a fish slice! I know right! It's daunting, but reader friend, don't be disheartened, please. There IS hope available and most of it is down to you. Own that son-of-a-bitch! Take control, but how? I hear you scream into the cold, black, empty dead of night. Two words, two words that shouldn't go together, shouldn't work, but do:

Sleep Hygiene.

No, you dumb ass, it doesn't mean taking your sleep for a shower (Wink emoji)

sleep hygiene

noun
noun: Sleep hygiene
habits and practices that are conducive to sleeping well on a regular basis."sleep hygiene is the key to sweet dreams"

Oh great, some more tree hugging hippy shit you have to deal with, wrong! This dippy, hippy shit is based on actual real science, conducted by actual real scientists. All probably wearing white lab coats and, incidentally, I bet they've all read a shit load of books and are all sexy and nerdy! Anyway, sleep hygiene. In a nut shell, for me anyway, is simply a series of things I do, or don't do, prior to bed, that helps let my body (and mind) know I'm going to bed, I'm going to sleep and to start doing my internal chemical rebalance. First off:

1. Listen to your body, which means listening to your body clock. Your entire body works off an internal clock, it's vital that this clock runs as smoothly as possible. I'm guessing if you've not skipped this chapter, yours is screwed up and you need it resetting. So how do you actually reset your body clock? Fortunately for you, I rang the help line and they suggested you switch it off and switch it back on again (for the benefit of me not getting sued, please do not do that and switch off your body al La Flatliners). What you can do are these few steps:

a. Get up at the same time every day. Yes, I said it! Every day Sunday through to Saturday baby, seven days a week. What this does is help to reset that fucking clock, and ironically, getting up at the same time every morning, helps make sure you go to bed at the same time every night. You'll find yourself getting tired and want to go to bed.

b. Remember number one? Listen to your body? Well, listen to your fucking body. If it's telling you it's tired, it's doing that for a reason, listen to it. Then, when you've listened to it, don't ignore it, go to bed.

c. Conversely, don't go to bed if you're not tired, unless a shag is on the cards. Going to bed and not going to sleep reinforces bad habits. Bad habits are not a good thing, that's why they are called BAD.

d. You are going to LOVE this one… NO technology for at least half an hour before your bed time. I know this one sucks, we are all hard wired now to keep our fucking phones in our hands until the very last second of consciousness, but imagine your phone wasn't a phone. Imagine it was a kaleidoscope. I bright, whirling, psychedelic explosion of colour, then imagine looking at that beautiful, retina burning, mass for half an hour and then I rock up and say:" Okay, time for bed". Now close your eyes, what are you going to see. It was a rhetorical question, we all know what you're going to see and that is why technology has to go. Besides, you can have it for the rest of the night, we're only talking 30 bloody minutes.

This also means no television, no radio, no stimuli at all for 30 minutes prior to bed, but what the hell are you going to do for 30 minutes before lights out?

i. Have a wank (cheeky)! Better still, if you've got someone else there, ask them to give you a wank. Don't go round to Geoff next door and ask him for a hand, I imagine he won't appreciate it and you'll end up in the ED department with swollen testicles (if you're a bloke) and a black eye, but your significant other should be able to help you out. If you're having no luck, show 'em this book, you can even highlight the following;

Dear significant other, although this is not, in any way shape or form, a Medical Certificate, I'd like you to consider giving your partner a quick five knuckle shuffle. They might not even want one really, but it's pretty much for medical purposes and the few minutes you spend on 'sorting them out' now, might just save their life later on. Go on, save a life today and get rubbing.

I hope that helped!

ii. Have a warm shower. Scrub the day off and get ready for the next day. Brush your teeth, Comb your hair, moisturise and chill.

iii. Meditate and by meditate, I mean sit in a quiet room, just focusing on your breathing. Don't think about anything else, other than your breathing, for about ten minutes. If you find your mind wondering, re-focus on your breathing. Set a timer, if you feel the need. No kids, TV, Partner, phone calls. Afford yourself absolutely no distractions of any kind and I promise you, you will feel better for it. We rarely allow ourselves the luxury of time, everyone is always so pushed for it, but it's vital that, for at least ten minutes a day, we turn our attention in on ourselves, solely and whole on ourselves.

There are literally thousands of books on sleep and meditation and there is a reason for that! Buy an app, a book a collection of dvd's, buy nothing at all, but DO focus on healthy sleep hygiene and meditation. Perhaps even incorporate one into the other! And your sleep will improve. You have to work at it and that work has to be consistent, but it will dividends in the long run.

Sleep tight.

AND A ONE, AND A TWO…

Exercise regularly

Blah blah blah! I knew he'd bang on about exercise eventually. Yes, it was something I was always going to touch on-because it's so fucking important. I'm not however, going to give you a training program, like I know what I'm talking about. I'll say find something you like, check with your doctor that's it's safe for you to do it. Start small and build up to your goal, BUT be consistent with it. Forty-five to sixty minutes of moderate to hard exercise, three times a day, is a very good place to start.

You thought there were a ton of books about sleep and meditation, try looking at books to get you healthy! Is it ironic that the two highest selling types of none-fiction books are exercise books and cook books?

What I will say is this, ENJOY what you're doing. It has to be enjoyable, or you won't stick with it, I guarantee one hundred percent. Try and pick something outside of a gym. I don't say this because I hate gyms. I love gyms and I belong to an absolutely brilliant one, and I adore going there and I work hard and I achieve great things, BUT with Covid, the gyms were open, then shut, then open, then shut, then open, then…. You get the picture. If you're running around your estate for forty-five minutes-no one can stop you, nothing can stop you and it's free!

Exercise, apart from making you healthy, is fucking awesome! You feel great and it's fun. Now, we whilst I'm not going to touch on what type of exercise you should be doing, I will talk about why you should be doing it. There are usually two camps; those who want to be healthy and those with a 'goal' loose weight, build muscle, reduce back and joint pain, and so on. I will say this and I've said it a thousand times-You cannot out exercise a bad diet. You can do all the sit ups and crunches you want, but if you're diet consists of beer and pies and lollies, you'll never see the result you're looking for.

I'll also say that, traditionally, most of the 'early' weight loss is down to water loss. That will fluctuate, don't be disheartened.

I'll also say fuck the scales. If you only look at the scales, numbers wise, Dwayne The Rock Johnston is clinically obese. Do you want to tell The Rock he's obese? Do you believe The Rock is obese? Of course he fucking isn't! Chances are though, if you weigh the same as The Rock and you don't actually look like The Rock, then I'm gonna guess you are obese, but hey, that's just a guess. Plus scales kill motivation. Monday through to Friday, you consistently lose 300 g a day, but on Saturday you have a blow out and you put on 500 g. I guarantee, you'll only focus on that half kilo gain, but do the math: 300 g a day over five days is a 1.5KG loss. You put 500 g back on, you've still lost 1KG. In a year, you could lose 52KG 1-52kg in a year, id say most people's goals would fall into that bracket, most, but what that means is that almost everyone's goals could be met within twelve months! But you have to be consistent. Consistent with your diet and consistent with your exercise. I personally like to mix things up as I get bored very easily. So I do upper and lower exercises, I do resistance training, alternating muscle groups, cardiac and a little yoga and stretch exercises to round things off. If the gym is open, I also like to do some swimming. I have a bad back (Poor me) and swimming is excellent, as it's a full body, none weight baring exercise.

If you want, find an exercise buddy. Someone to bare the load with, share the struggles and share the achievements. Set yourself some goals, make yourself accountable. Run 1 kilometre without crying! Run five. Do a 15K fun run? Bench press your own body weight, swim 20 lengths. It could be anything, but goals really do help focus the mind. Plus if you're doing a charity thing, you don't want to fail and look like a complete dick!

So ditch the scales, your weight will always change, up to a kilogram a day, due to time of the month, water retention, if you've not taken a crap, what you ate and when you ate it. What won't lie to you is if your pants feel baggy or tight! Do NOT but bigger clothes, ever! You are lying to yourself and you'll get Orca fat!

Fat, fat, fat, fat, fat fat. Fattie fatties bum bum, fat. Fattity, fattity, fat fat!

It's okay to say fat! Some ultra modern branch of society will tell me it's cruel to use the word fat. It's body shaming and the word shouldn't be used. It's not 'helpful' and degenerating. I don't think you should call someone ugly or short or specie-four-eyes. You can't do anything about your looks, we're all beautiful in our own way. You can't make yourself taller, any more that you can change the need to wear glasses, but you can do something about being over weight and to try and PC sugar coat it into something it isn't doesn't help either. Now, I do think you can call yourself fat, your personal trainer can too, although they shouldn't, but the guy sat next to you on the bus shouldn't be able to, that's just not necessary and is totally fat shaming someone, and should never be tolerated.

Oh, one last thing: You're not 'big boned' NO ONE is big boned, you are fat. You are fat because you over eat shite food and don't exercise. You do not have a glandular problem, that makes you put on 40 kg too heavy. You are fat and lazy. If you try and tell me you exercise for an hour a day and only eat salad and you're still over weight, then you are lying to me and/or you are lying to yourself. Enough of the bullshit excuses already, man up, or person up. Take ownership. Take charge. Take control. This is YOUR body, this is your choice, your decision. You can be the better version of yourself, but no one can do it for you. Someone else can help you, many people can help you. If you have a shit load of money, you could have a chef and a personal trainer and all that shit, but chances are, with Covid right now, you couldn't see them at all, so best to do it yourself. Go for a run (free) do sit ups and push ups (free). Hell, you can even google free HIIT training video and do a none equipment based exercise program f.o.r f.r.e.e! Fine, but tell me more about diet……. Fine!

H TWO OH, I SEE

Drink more water and eat well

In the real world, I'm a nurse. I've been a nurse for almost thirty years. I'm a Scrub/Scout peri-operative nurse in a busy operating theatres and, on occasion, I scrub for surgery that is complex and time consuming-three/four hours long, sometimes longer. If you told me to drink three litres of water a day, so I'm pissing like a diabetic camel, how the hell am I supposed to do that and still work? Or I'm a road train driver, or one of another thousand jobs? Well, the truth is, I do drink around 2.5 litres a day and whilst I was pissing like a leaky tap for the first couple of days, my body soon found its own, new normal and needing to take a leak soon became a problem of the past. It's estimated that around 98 percent of the population of the planet is, to one degree or another, is dehydrated! Ninety-eight percent! That's insane.

You ask Doctor Google on the old internet how much water you should drink a day, it says:

The US National Academies of Sciences, Engineering, and Medicine determined that an adequate daily fluid intake is: About **15.5 cups (3.7 litres) of fluids a day for men**. **About 11.5 cups (2.7 litres) of fluids a day for women.**14 Oct 2020

Men, almost FOUR litres! They might be right, but Jesus Christ our Lord and Saviour! Four litres! I don't think I could do it. I can do two, at a push, if I'm a day off work and I know where all the toilets are, but four litres on a work day-that's not happening love, not for me anyway. I will, however, do my best and if doing my best means 2.1 or 2.2, I'll be happy with that. I might find once I hit 2.2, it gets easier and 4 litres isn't actually too bad, but my brain and my bladder ain't there yet.

Truth is, if you just make little improvements daily, you're making daily improvements and daily improvements are 100% better than daily failures, just do your best.

Water is, essentially, just about volume. You'll manage it or you won't. Food, on the other hand, is a complete sweaty ball sack of a pain in the ass. Where do you even begin with diet and who the hell am I to talk about them any way? Well, in the same way I know how I like my eggs cooked, but I'm not a chef, that's how. I know what has worked for me and I know what has not. 100%, no messing around, I'll tell you what doesn't work "Diets". Diets are, in essence, short term solutions to long term problems. You can't eat lettuce today, so you can eat chocolate tomorrow, it just doesn't work.

Likewise, you could tell me the only thing I'd have to give up to lose 30Kg was sprouts and I guarantee, the first thing I'd want would be a bowl of sprouts. That's just how my brain works. You cannot demonise a food group. You cannot say carbs are evil, we need carbs. We just need the right carbs at the right time. Some people swear by intermittent fasting, some by meal replacement shakes, some by pre-packed meals. Pretty much everything that works, works because of one principle: Calories in Vs calories out. There are a thousand ways to calculate your daily calorie allowance, but in essence, it works like this; to just maintain your body, breathing, digestive system, brain function, walking, all that shit. That all takes fuel, so, for the sake of this argument and math, Let's say me, as a bloke, I need 3000 calories a day, just to function. If I only take in 2000 calories from food and drink, I'll need to 'find' the other 1000 calories and since I have a reserve of fat cells and fat is essentially unused, reserved energy, my body will use those cells to enhance the 2000 calories I'm bringing in via food, to make up the deficit.Therefore, your body uses it's own fat for energy, you lose weight!

That's a very, very over simplified way of looking at it, but the principle is solid. Find your daily allowance and figure out your calories in vs calories out. Add into that, at least one hours of moderate exercise 3-4 days a week and you'll be rocking the kind of summer body that doesn't need airbrushing or filters in no time at all, but if you sneak 5-6 chocolate biscuits at night, or a bag of chips, or a beer or two, then you're fucked. You have no chance and you'll never achieve your goals.

You could go live in the 'fuck it' camp. Fuck it people are cool, for a little while, cos they seem like they have their shit together and, obviously, don't sound like they give an actual fuck about what you think or what you say. The fuck it, I'm fat. Fat is what I am and I ain't gonna change for no mother fucker and if you don't like it, you can sit on my stubby little fat dick, kind of person and whilst it's cool to be cool, one day your fat body will fail you. Your knees will hurt, your back will ache, you'll get out of breath walking to the fridge for cheese, it'll take you fifteen minutes to put on your God damned socks, you'll stop fucking, you'll get chest pains and anxiety. You'll stop taking your shirt off at the beach, then you'll stop going to the beach, then you'll stop going out, or talking to people. You'll do on line shopping, watch Russian porn and troll people on the internet, all from your mother's basement, that you can't get out of, because you are too fucking fat and you know it. If that's how you want to live your life, I am NOT here to tell you otherwise, if that brings you happiness, then so be it, but if you are NOT happy, I'm here to tell you it's okay to change. It's okay to want to change. It's okay to do something, or what to do something that you think will make your life better.

Where do you start? What do you do? You do one thing, just one thing. You can't go from a sedentary life, eating cake and pies and shit to totally organic, exercising for three hours a day, seven days a week. Is it possible? Sure, but I don't believe that's a sustainable model. You'll give up, eat more shit, because you feel bad, and end up being worse off than before. Better to make one small change, nail that, then move on to the next one. It might be don't drink fizzy drinks Monday to Thursday, only buy one take out meal a week. After a week, you'll do something else, I guarantee it (As long as you've not cheated). If you have cheated, it's okay. You know you're only cheating on yourself, and where is the fun in that?

Small changes.
Set goals.
Tell everyone you're doing it.
Be accountable.
Be prepared to fail and try again.
Stop buying sweatpants that are two sizes too big for you, they don't look half as good as you think they do

You got this.

ANYONE GOT A LIFE JACKET?

Ask for help

This one is simple, but by no means short; ask for help you dick. I don't care what it is that's bothering you. Fact is, something is bothering you and that's gotta stop. I don't care how much your ego is gonna get bruised. I don't care if you've got to talk to a parent you've not spoken to for years, ask for help.

I'm amazed how bone headed and stupid we can be in this world, and I should know, I used to be that person. I wouldn't ask nobody for nothing. I know that's bad now, but at the time, I was convinced there was no way anyone would or could help. I thought no one would understand and I knew in the marrow of my bones no one could possibly relate to my issues. There's the thing, once I got to talking about my shit, I realised I couldn't have been more wrong about every single one of those things, I mean every single one! You ask the right person for help-it's gonna change your life!

There are a swathe of places to get help: Lifeline, Beyond Blue, Headtohelp, and a dozen more I've not mentioned (Sorry). Your GP will know who to refer you to, let them help.

Why do you even need someone to talk to? Well, on the Australian governments own website, they state that in 2019 there were 3,318 suicide deaths in Australia alone. 816 of those were by females and 2,502 were by males! Men are three times more likely than women to commit suicide and do you know why? I'm gonna take a wild guess on this one. A girl gets upset, for the most part, they talk to someone; their mom, their sister, best friend, whoever, they talk to someone. A man gets upset, who does he talk to? No one! Not a single soul. Why? Because if he talks to someone, it makes him weak, he's a pussy and a failure and he'll never recover from the shame of asking for help. He'll be a social outcast and deservedly so- what a crock of shit. You know who would have benefited from having someone to talk to? Those 2,502 poor souls who took their own lives in 2019 because talking would make them less of a man.

I will talk to anyone about anything. I'm a damned, un-closable, open book. I am open and honest and brutally so. You get me talking, you'll eventually get round to telling me to shut the fuck up, why? Because I've learned, over time, that talking helps. I mean it really helps. I don't have a huge circle of friends, but I true ones I have. When I've had to deal with 'stuff' bigger than our friendship can accommodate, I've spoken in therapy and it is liberating. None judgemental, respectful communication. You know what happened when I first opened up? Nothing! Fuck all! The sky didn't fall in, the ground didn't open up and swallow me whole. My friends and family didn't scream and run for the hills. I just felt better, I felt unburdened. That's me though, that might not be you. As an example, I'm going to go with the 'problem' I probably see the most in movies, the one where the son is gay, he tells his parents and one, or both, of them disapproves and kicks them out of the house for being a sinner or whatever.

Firstly, if you're gay, well you belong to a massive community already. It is estimated that ten percent of our population is gay, as of 2019, the population of Australia is 25.36 million, ten percent of that is 2,536000. One in a hundred people are, statistically, gay. That does not take into account the rest of the LGBTIQA+ community and before I go any further, lets unpeel that, a little.

Lesbian, Gay, Bisexual, Transgender, Queer or Questioning, Intersex and Allies

Anyway, back to the 2,502 males who took their own lives in 2019. How many of those, do you think, would still be with us today if they'd have talked to someone about what was troubling them? I know that talking isn't always the answer, I know deep, deep depression can take you, no matter how surrounded with people, or supported you are, to a very, very dark place, but I have to believe that, I don't know.... 60% of those men who didn't talk to someone, MIGHT have benefited from being able to talk to someone. If you're the gay guy who feels alone, mate there are 2.5 million of you in Australia alone, 1 in 100 people are gay, you are surrounded by other gay people. You just have to find your tribe, they will welcome you. Now, this is where it gets tricky for me, because I've never had to find that tribe before. I know about some of the 'dating' apps and some will help you find true love and some will help you find the next cock to suck, choose accordingly.

There are a ton of social media communities, for example, dedicated to gay support groups. In fact, there are support groups for all aspects of the LGBTIQA+ community (I may have to explain a few of these internet searches to my wife), but with just the briefest of internet searches, I found a mountain of help. If you belong to this community and feel alone, trust me, you are not!

If you're a straight person looking to help, I did some research on your behalf, you're welcome, and found a few tips, like these:

Listen to the person explaining their lives and respect it. It is their life and they know how they want to live it. 'It' might be a phase, it might also be a realisation of who they are. It's not a 'choice,' you can't choose to be gay or bisexual etc, any more than you can chose how tall you are, or the colour of your eyes (I always wanted Paul Newman Blue damn it!) And whoever is talking to you has gone through a world of fucking internal and external turmoil to get to the point where they have the courage to talk, that's some next level brave shit right there, as far as I'm concerned and that bravery should be celebrated.

Speak up when you hear someone talking shit. I'm half Irish and I've spent my entire life listening to fucking Irish jokes. I still laugh at most jokes, because they are funny, but you hear someone call a friend, family member or fuck it, even a stranger, a faggot, poof or other name, see someone ill treated because of who they are, you fucking well speak up. Your best friend is getting pushed around in the locker room after gym for being a 'fag,' you stand between him and his aggressors, stare them dead in the eyes and tell them to fuck off! Bullying, especially from your peers, does increase rates of depression, anxiety and suicide and can lead to absolutely devastation.

Respect the pronouns. I get confused as shit about this, it's not my generations way of talking, but I've slowly educated myself, as best I can and I try really hard to get it right. I fuck up sometimes, when that happens, one of two things occur, I either apologise and use the right pronoun or the person with whom I'm talking, corrects me and I apologise and use the right pronoun. Why is it important? Imagine you're a bloke called John Smith and every time someone talks to you, they call you Miss Smith. Would that annoy you? Would it piss you off? Why should it? It's only a word right, fuck sake, get over it! No, that shit would eventually really piss you off, because how people are identifying you, isn't how you identify yourself and how you identify yourself is critical to who you are. So if someone wants the pronouns they and them, well then fucking well use those pronouns, it won't kill you and it shows respect!

Back to the kid who hasn't got that. The kid who feels alone, broken, isolated, different. What happens to him? Well, if he don't get support or continues to feel alone, there's a good chance he's going to end up one of those statistics. I don't want that. I don't want that for anyone, so please ask for help! If your parents won't listen or want to change you or sign you up to conversion therapy classes, them fuck 'em, they are so not worth your effort. You can't pray the gay away any more than you can therapy the gay away and your parents are fucking idiots. Besides, your problems might not have anything to do with your sexuality and honestly, if the most interesting thing about you is your sexuality, then you need a fucking hobby. You are NOT your sexuality, your sexuality is part of you, not the other way around. You might need help because you're struggling in school, you can't make friends easily, you are bipolar or have A.D.D or dyslexia. You might even, God forbid, be ginger! In which case, there is no hope for you. You might as well run away and join the circus now! (Please don't run off and join the circus, that was just a joke and you are loved, even when you are ginger.)

Point is, no one can help you with anything, if you don't speak up. Speaking up is hard, it might be the hardest thing you've ever had to do. It will make you vulnerable, you might be scared or feel alone, isolated and it might be painfully different and awkward, but I promise you 100%, there is a world of people out there who feel exactly the same and as long as you talk to the right people, you'll never feel worse for having spoken. Reach out, find a friendly ear and spill your guts.

PEACE OFF

Meditation, is the name of the game
verb
verb: meditate; 3rd person present: meditates; past tense: meditated; past participle: meditated; gerund or present participle: meditating.

focus one's mind for a period of time, in silence or with the aid of chanting, for religious or spiritual purposes or as a method of relaxation."I set aside time every day to write and meditate"

- think deeply about (something)."he went off to meditate on the new idea"

Listen, I'm not talking about sitting atop a mountain range listening to the rain fall, or in the middle of a desert, but I guess we need to figure out WHY you should meditate long before we consider HOW to meditate. Truth is, we live in a noisy world, a really fucking noisy world and we are constantly bombarded with stimuli. From the moment we wake, to the moment we collapse onto our beds exhausted at night, it is constant, persistent and relentless and truth is, sometimes we need to switch ourselves off from all that constant white noise. I mean, sometimes we really need to switch ourselves off from it and that, as we all know, is not easy.

It is relentless. Think about it, when was the last time you actually just sat down, in silence and did nothing? We are saturated by it, or our desire for it, or our conditioning for it! To use a cinematic metaphor, we need to unplug from The Matrix once in a while and whilst that can be hard, I promise you, it will be worth it.

I used to be the kind of person who would scoff at meditation, no seriously. I mean full on scoff! I would take the piss out of it, without really knowing what it was or what it meant, or what it could achieve. I had this pre-formed picture of not only what meditation was, but also what type of person did it. You know, blokes with man buns who drank soy lattes and over energetic, stay at home mums in bright pink gym wear who never actually went to the gym, BUT that all changed once I dipped my unenthusiastic toe in the pool of meditation. I'd now consider meditation vial. Doing it really opened my eyes, well actually it closed my eyes, but you know what I mean.

So why do I meditate? Well, first off, read above, secondly:

Boffins in white coats somewhere have scientifically shown that meditation decreases stress. It does this by lowering your stress hormone Cortisol. Cortisol is, when properly released by our bodies, a great hormone, but like most hormones, it becomes an issue when our systems go Kerfluie and doesn't interact with our bodies in the way it is supposed to. Increases in Cortisol increased stress and anxiety and depression! Bad Hormone!

When you're anxious or stressed out and someone slaps you across the face, a little too aggressively if you ask me, and shouts "Pull yourself together man" and you stop and breath and rethink your situation, what you just did there was self regulate a stressful situation with mindfulness and a deeper state of mindfulness is meditation! Ta-Dar! Meditation just helped you deal with stress in a more mindful way, which leads to:

Mood boosts. Think about it, you just became way less stressed. Being way less stressed HAS to put you in a better mood because you just made things better and you can't make things better and we in a worse mood! Try it, I dare you, I double dare you. Do something that makes you happier and try and be in a worse mood, go on, I'll wait……

You couldn't do it could you. That was a rhetorical question, I already know the answer. You can't, so meditation puts you in a better mood, which means, by definition, you also decrease anxiety and reduce the risk of depression… Say what now? ALL from ten minutes of meditation a day! Shut up and take my money.

As your cortisol levels drop, your serotonin levels increase. Spotty kid at the back of the class:
"Professor O'Toole, as a world renowned scientist, can you tell us what an increase in serotonin does?"

I can, even though I am neither a professor or a scientist! It is a natural mood stabiliser, which, and (I'm gonna use a big scientific statement here people, so buckle in! It helps to chill you the fuck out!

But what does that do to our cardiovascular system, third person Gary? Meditation has been shown to decrease the risk of cardiovascular disease. It positively impacts heart muscle effectiveness, generally improves cardiovascular mortality and helps lower high blood pressure.

Thats just some of the physical benefits to meditation, but what about the emotional, psychological and, dare I say it, spiritual benefits? Meditation allows you to experience stillness. Most of us are not comfortable with stillness. We feel like we have to be 'on' or doing something. Once you become comfortable with the stillness of meditation, you will be able to draw down from that experience and apply it to 'normal' life.

You'll be better at concentrating, which makes sense, as you'll be actively working at concentrating for at least ten minutes a day. You'll develop the mental equivalent of muscle memory. You will learn to centre your mind and remain focused and mentally alert. This also allows us to be more present in 'the moment'. The moment sounds very wanky, I know and I'm writing this! But it really does. You have to be switched on, mentally, to meditate, to be mindful enough to make that conscious decision to meditate. Your thoughts will be more focused and clarity breeds clean, decisive thoughts and actions.

Sometimes, when my wife leaves for work before me, she'll wake me up to say goodbye and then tell me twenty things I have to do around the house. Once she's gone and I'm awake, I'm like what the fuck just happened and what the hell did she just say? I know she rattled off three or four jobs for me to do and I'll be lucky if I remember one! That living nightmare is like trying to un-scramble eggs! It's a brain fog you can never lift. Meditation cannot help me with my list of wife chores, but it can help with general brain fog. As already stated, meditation can bring stillness to a busy mind and clarity to a fogged one. Concentration, forgetfulness, indecision. All of those issues, and more, can be helped by just sitting fucking still for ten minutes! Show me an exercise that does as much as meditation does in ten minutes! You won't be able to, it doesn't exist. Except for that one where you sit on an invisible chair, resting against a wall, that one fucking kills!

Meditation helps with pain management, insomnia, helps with your immune system, reduces inflammation, improves mental function, it can help you lose weight and better and a hundred more things. Can we just get over ourselves and acknowledge that meditation is, over all and without exception, a good thing and move on?

So we now know we want to meditate-yes, you, you want to meditate now, okay, but what type of meditation are you gonna go with? How do you even find out what types of meditation there are and which would suit you?

Well, thank you once again Mr Google.

mindfulness meditation
spiritual meditation
focused meditation
movement meditation
mantra meditation
transcendental meditation
progressive relaxation
Loving-kindness meditation

I particularly like the sound of loving-kindness meditation because some people are dumb as rocks and give me the shits! However, before you pick the mind-fuckiest of forms of meditation, can I humbly suggest you go with the simplest of styles and go from there.

First off, find somewhere to sit comfortably, without the fear of disruption for fifteen minutes. For example, sitting at the dining room table, whilst the kids are playing and the TV is on is, perhaps, not the best setting. How about your bedroom, with the door closed and with everyone strict instructions to leave you the fuck alone for fifteen minutes. Better still, do it whilst your partner is at work and the ankle biters are at school (if you're not still home schooling them right through to fucking University)
Make sure you have a note pad and pen, I will explain why shortly.

Time to slip into some baggy pants and a loose fitting top. You don't have to look like a Shar-Pei (The dog, not the pen!) But you do have to be comfortable.

Sit down. Floor is great, but you can sit anywhere, as long as you are sat upright and you are sat without back support (IF possible). I like to sit on the edge of the bed. I'm comfortable, but well supported.

Now, close your eyes and focus solely on your breathing and just your breathing. You know, breath in… breath out…

You might find your mind actively distracts you, shopping lists, what to have for dinner, what to watch on tv tonight, where did you put that bill you had to pay? That kind of crap, but if your mind does this, take the note pad and pen and write down what's distracting you. Just dump those thoughts right onto the pad and move them out of your brain. Empty your mind of all thoughts, for some reason it's easier for men to do than women that one, go figure. Move all that noise out and just focus on the breathing. If you find your mind wondering, just bring it back to the breathing. You might have a positive affirmation, you might want to listen to some music, just music mind, nothing with lyrics, they'll distract you.

The first few times, you'll catch yourself thinking, even before you've registered you're thinking and that is perfectly normal. It might be quite some time before you stop doing this and that's okay too. This technique will be new to you and it might take you some time to master it. It might not, you might be one of those annoying pricks who just slide right into it with no problems at all, I hate you and everything you stand for! I don't obviously, we all take the time we need, to achieve the goals we want to achieve and this skill is no different. What I will say is, like all skills, the more you do it, the more adept at it you will become.

Give it ten minutes a night, every night for a week and see if it makes a difference. Spoiler Alert: It will make a difference and your mind will blown by just how much.

YOU BE DOCTOR, I'LL BE NURSE

Kids remember, play makes you immortal (Kind of).

This is all about fun really. I found, as I got older and my responsibilities grew, my ability to just have fun shrunk back into the shadows. I mean, I could still have fun, of course, but I was equally concerned with paying the bills, doing well at work, putting the kids through a better schooling system than the one I had, and it was a little exhausting if I'm being completely honest.

When I was a younger man, I was fearless. Literally devoid of fear, nothing concerned me and I was game for anything. There are two types of people in this world, those who cannonball into the pool and hope there is water there, and those who need to know how deep the water is, its temperature and its viscosity. I was never that person, I was always the former, but as time and life and circumstances went by, I started to morph into the latter and that bugged the crap out of me, so I'd dance in the Streets, tell terrible jokes, splash in puddles and maintained, where possible, a youthful disposition. I'm not talking about being childish here, although that can be fun too. I'm talking about remaining present, relevant, self aware and confident. I truly believe an old mind helps create an old body, and when your body is old, you are fucked.

There are exceptions, of course, there always are. I have some age related changes I can't avoid, but how much of those changes are age related and how many of them are changes I could have avoided, had I made different choices in my life? If I kept doing gymnastics, perhaps I'd be more flexible than I am and perhaps I wouldn't now be over weight? Well, that was never going to happen, mostly because I never did gymnastics! But I did box and weight train. If I'd have kept that up, perhaps I'd look like The Rock instead of Shrek, but I optimistically believe I can still make the required changes to get me to achieve the goals I've set myself and you can do the same. I'm fifty-five now and still looking forward to the future. I intend to get to seventy-five and still looking forward to being ninety-five. Now, I might not get to ninety-five, but I guarantee I'll be happier when I reach the end than someone who was dreading it. It's about maintaining a positive mental attitude because that positive mental attitude will keep you going, long after everyone else has turned to dust.

The most important thing is, don't act your age, remember to play. Play hide and seek, throw a Frisbee down the beach and do something outside of work. You have to have something to look forward to, you have to have goals. Like a shark, keep moving forward (only, you know, without the blood and death). We've all heard the horror stories about 'Geoff', but do you want to be the Geoff who spent fifty years at the same company and when he retired, two weeks later dropped down dead from a heart attack, or do you want to be Geoff who spent fifty years at the same company and when he retired, happily spent the next twenty years tending to his beloved garden, meeting up with his friends from the bowling green for morning coffee and took up still life painting? I sure as shit know which one I'd prefer to be and deep down, I think you do too.

So how can you actively work towards a brighter future? Well, as it turns out, quite a lot.

Firstly, forget everything you think you know about ageing and the stereotypes society has attached to it. Old people ageing; stooped over, walking slow with a stick or a frame, thick glassed, hearing aid and a miserable attitude that could piss off even the Devil himself is NOT normal ageing, that's abnormal ageing, THAT'S the mutation, not the other way around. If you associate ageing with traditional ageing words like grumpy, senile or weak, then a person is going to be grumpy, senile and/or weak, but if you use words like active, sharp, knowledgable, then guess what…? Millions of people are aged, hardly any of them fall into true stereotype. So if they don't fall into true stereotype, what makes that the stereotype to fall into in the first place? And can I get through this paragraph without having to spell stereotype again? Damn it!

Secondly, remember Geoff and dropping down dead? Make a list, way before you retire, and DO IT! The list could be physical; run a marathon or redesign your garden. Cognitive; learn Japanese to take up crosswords. My career goal is to hit sixty-five and go work at a big, national hardware store here in Australia. I LOVE this hardware store and I'm really excited at the prospect of eventually working there. Right now, I am learning to play the Ukulele, I'm learning basic life drawing skills, Indian cookery, mobile photography, singing, the best way to use acrylic paints, fitness and nutrition, how to create and run an Amazon Wholesale business and I'm doing a complete beginners course on basic dance moves for men. I've written 26 children's books, a cook book, two novels and one book about how not to be a dick, I have a full time job and two kids under sixteen. Oh and I'm learning how to knit. Did I mention I like to learn new stuff and keep myself busy? I could quit my job tomorrow and still have enough in the day to fill the day three times over. There is no way I'm getting 'old'. When I drop down dead, I'm going out 'young'. I'd like to suggest you do the same.

SPACE, THE FINAL LUXURY

Your partner is not your life
This one is a Carolina Reaper Chilli. Short, but ferociously flavoured.

This is a direct follow on from the previous chapter. Let me get one thing straight, right off the bat, before I end up with a bread knife in my chest, I love my wife. We have been together, as of 2021, almost thirty years and my life wouldn't be the same without her, but we do not live in each others pockets. I would drive her absolutely insane! We allow ourselves time and space to be individuals, to be something other than 'The husband" or "The wife" or 'The parent". We enjoy these roles and relish our time together and as a family unit, but it's not all that we are. If we spent every minute of every day in each others company, what would there be left to talk about? I'd say Hey wife, guess what happened to me today and she'd be like, I know exactly what happened to you today stupid, I was there next to you. We'd end up having nothing to talk about and that would be sad (and problematic). By giving each other a little bit of space and the opportunity to maintain a modicum of individuality, we keep everything fresh and alive and vibrant.

We have friends we can catch up with, well my wife has friends, I just write about having them and I think we've managed to find a reasonably good balance. My wife is very shy, but sociable. I'm very out going, but strangely, being sociable, for me, can sometimes be problematic, even with my wife to guide me. Sometimes I just need to be people free for a while, and in all honesty, at those times, I'm not worth being around anyway, but my wife recognises that in me and gives me the space I need to wrestle with my monsters, if and when they rear their ugly heads. If she didn't, or I didn't, we'd soon feel suffocated in the relationship.

We are more than the sum of our parts and even if you got married at twenty, you still had twenty years, give or take, of being your own person, it's important you don't lose that sense of individuality, after all, isn't that what your partner fell in love with?

The key phrase here is Me Time and trust me, everyone needs it. Imagine your partner is the most delicious cupcake you've ever tasted, (go with me on this one). You love that cupcake, it's got the perfect balance between sweet and salty, light and crunchy. There's just the right amount of filling and the frosting is whipped so light and airy, it's like eating candy floss. It is perfection on a plate. Now imagine getting that cake rammed down your throat twenty-four/seven. Even if it was the best cupcake you'd ever encountered, you'd soon feel queasy, then you'd get the sugar sweats, then you'd collapse, vomit and develop type II diabetes! How much do you love that cupcake now?

The worse thing you can do is define yourself by the relationship you are currently in, your partner is not the only thing about you that is interesting and remember, you absolutely do not have to like the same things all the time. I love the movies and a good show tune. My wife enjoys a great book and streaming shows. You can play the "Do you remember when…?" game all the live, long day, but that will soon get boring very, very quickly, best you go off and create some new memories together, and apart and then you've actually got something to talk about.

THROW THAT SHIT OUT

De-clutter

I think I've mentioned this before, but it's worth repeating, I say to my wife all the time, that I'm going to the shops to spend money we don't have, on shit we don't need. I literally say it all the time, and why do I say it? Because we love buying shit, but de-clutter isn't just about curbing your spending, it's so much more. So, first off, let's deal with the house situation. I could be wrong, it wouldn't be the first or last time, but let's imagine, for a moment, that you don't live in a house waiting to be photographed from a glamour magazine. Let's imagine that you house is a 'normal' house, filled with stuff, how much of that stuff do you really need? If the idea of de-cluttering your house is way too fucking daunting, how about we start small, or literally with your smalls! Let's start with your sock draw. I got news for you guys, there ain't a woman alive who finds holes in socks attractive, they just ain't. Equally, there is nothing alluring about a pair of sweaty old jocks with broken elastic, holes and skid marks! I mean there's always a possibility, I guess, for some twisted sub-culture who digs that shit, but I've not found it because I'm not looking! Throw that shitty stuff out, just throw it out, burn it, bury it, send in into outer space, just get rid. Go down to a store, or shop on line and buy yourself some brand spanking new underwear and/or socks, and when you put them on for the first time, remember that feeling, because you will feel magical. Now style, that's up to you of course, boxer, briefs, trunks, whatever makes you feel sexy and confident and YES I do mean blokes here. There is no reason, on God's green Earth, that you can't feel confident and sexy, even at work. A person should always feel these things. Feeling sexy doesn't make you more sexual, what it does is it super charges your confidence levels, because who's ever met anyone who's sexy and NOT confident? There's a reason for that.

So, you've taken out all your odd socks, your socks with holes and your jocks that are threadbare from all that ass scratching and, with fully ramped up irony, don't your draws look better! Don't you feel more confident? Now, you see what you just did with those torn up old skids? Go into your wardrobe and do the same! That's right, march in there right now and if you've got something you've not worn for a year in there, put it in a big old bag and mark it "Charity Shop" and continue. Take everything out, tees, pants, jumpers, shirts, the lot. That tee shirt you've been holding onto for three fucking years, because you're 'gonna' fit into it again one day! Dude! You ain't, stop fucking fooling yourself and even if you get to a size where that tee is gonna fit you again, who wants to wear a three year old teeshirt? Same with pants, if you've got a 112 cm waste and you're still hoping to get into those 90 cm jeans…… You may want to reconsider that? I'm not saying it isn't going to happen, and if it's something you want to achieve, I totally hope you achieve your goal (Seriously, we have the same goal) but manage your expectations a little and let those fucking jeans go to a better home! Now you've done your sock and pants draw(s) and your wardrobe, there should be no stopping you. Old pans that everything sticks to, plastic tubs with no lids, chipped cups, rusty scissors, anything-throw-that-shit-out! Tidy the home office, do some filing, do some shredding. Tidy your desk, empty the waste bin, clear the clutter. If you're like me, the biggest areas where the shit piling philosophy really kicks in, is either the garden and/or the garage!

My garage is a black-fucking-hole of shit magnetism! If it's shite, it's going in my garage, and if you have a wife like mine, everything will be dumped 3 cm from the hall door, so even if you wanted to, you couldn't get in there if you tried. Here is what you do in that situation, you hire a skip. They are usually modestly priced, more so if you hire them at the weekend, when the Monday to Friday tradies are not using them. They get dropped off, they get picked up! There are a few rules and regulations about what you can and cannot put in them, but that will all be explained. I love a good skip clear out, it holds no prisoners.

"What should I do with this?"

"Put it in the Skip"

"What should I do with this?"

"Put it in the Skip"

"What should I do with this?"

"Put it in the Skip"

Or better still, sell the fucking thing and make some cash, only don't buy more shit with the cash!

Until there is no more shit left. Now, even in the garage, you have to be brutal. No saving that piece of wood 'just in case' or that collection of jam jars because you might make jam again in four years, throw those fucking things away!

Now you have a nice, neat, tidy and organised house. Take a deep breath, you did amazing.

Now take another deep breath, because the work has only just begun….

De-cluttering isn't just about stuff and things, it's about you. It's about internally de-cluttering, people and thoughts and relationships that are not doing you any good are, by definition, doing you harm. It's about time you addressed that, right!

Let's talk about me, hypothetically. Say I had a friend and I told that friend I wanted to be a writer, and that friend say dude, (because I'm dope and all my friends say dude, or am I fly? I'll have to google it), what you want to try do something like that for? You know how many people try to be writers and fail? Best you don't even try, put that shit to bed man, live your life free of all that stress and anguish bro'. If I'd have listened to that friend, would you be reading this book right now? I don't think so, see some 'friends' have a picture of who you are in their heads and what you mean to them and that's never going to change, and their subconscious philosophy is, if I'm not going to change, you shouldn't either. They like who you are and want you to remain being that person , but you can change, and if you want to change, then that's definitely what you should do, and no 'friend' would try and stop you. Now if someone does try and stop you, they are, probably, doing it out of love, not spite and if they are doing it out of love, do you really want to cut them out of your life? Well, if you tell them what you want and why you want it, and they still don't support you then yes, they have to go, or at the very least, sidelined until you get what you need because I promise you, they will drip doubt into your ear until that's all you can focus on. They will distract you from your goal, because your goal isn't their goal and once you fail, they will offer you support. They will tell you they knew they were right and that you were, obviously, going to fail and although that's a shame, they are always there for you bro. Hot tip! They are not there for you, they are there for themselves. They don't have your best interest at heart, they have theirs, and if they have their interests at heart, and not yours, why give them any more of your time?

De-cluttering is hard. It's actively letting go of something you've tried incredibly hard to hold on to for so long, but ultimately, letting go of all that clutter will be the best thing to do and deep, deep down… you know it too. I don't care who it is, a parent, a brother/sister, a partner, a friend. If a person in your life doesn't want the absolute best for you, why have them in your life? I know what I'm saying, I know how harsh that sounds. It sounds harsh because it is harsh, but that doesn't mean I'm wrong, right.

Sometimes the people who want the best for us, don't actually want the best for us! How fucked up is that? De-clutter as much of your life as possible. You have a credit card and all you can do each month is pay off the minimum, because you maxed it out four years ago and now you're screwed? Go talk to your bank, tell them you want out of that fucking hole and you'd like their help doing it. De-clutter your house, your mind, your bank balance and your credit cards. De-clutter your pantry and the filing cabinet in your office. De-clutter your wardrobe, your book shelf, your contact list and your life. Start small, finish big. The difference it will make to your life is immeasurable, because once you de-clutter, once you've found and activated that mindset, it's really difficult to switch it off. You'll faulted and fail a few times for sure, but once you 'get it' you've got it and you'll be off. There are numerous books on the subject and I highly recommend reading a few, only once you've read them, get rid of them!

HOW TO AVOID THE C-SPOT

Comfort zones are not comfortable.
"Your comfort zone will kill you"
Sam Smith (Instagram 2021)
Forget the damned comfort zone, but Gary, I hear you ask, what the hell is a comfort zone and why are you so fundamentally opposed to it? Why reader, those are a couple of excellent questions, ones I feel deserving of an answer. comfort zone

Comfort Zone
noun

a situation where one feels safe or at ease."the trip is an attempt to take the students out of their comfort zone"
a settled method of working that requires little effort and yields only barely acceptable results."if you stay within your comfort zone you will never improve"

Them there, those are direct sections of The Oxford English Dictionary and within those two sentences, you know everything you need to know about what a comfort zone is, and why it's so bad for you…

A situation where one feels at ease and you yield only barely acceptable results. Do you want to coast through life, generating only barely acceptable results? You see, whilst you are in your comfort zone, being all warm and cosy and safe, there are other people outside of their, kicking ass and scoring goals. The comfort zone is like the paddling pool at the gym, everyone else is doing full ass Olympic lengths in the big boy pool, and there you are, with your inflatable arm rings, splashing about like damn idiot in the paddle pool! You ain't going nowhere, you are treading water:

Tread water
phrase of tread

maintain an upright position in deep water by moving the feet with a walking movement and the hands with a downward circular motion."they were at the deep end of the pool and trod water to keep afloat"

fail to make progress."men who are treading water in their careers"

Fail to make progress. Do you consider yourself to be the kind of person who fails to make progress? The kind of person who barely does enough to keep their head above the water? Are you the kind of person who absolutely refuses to better themselves and excel in whatever it is you are doing, to shine, like a beacon of light for anyone and everyone who dares to look up to you and your achievements? Because if that is you, then stop reading this book right now and go give it to someone who'll actually benefit from owning it.

You have to step outside of your comfort zone, nothing grows there, it's cold and dark and lonely, step into the light, where it is warm and bright and fun and everything grows. You need to be free of that comfort zone bad. Here's the thing, you know if you're going to succeed right? I mean, you know better than anyone.
You know you're going to do it, no matter what that 'it' is, but you also know that, in order to achieve 'it,' you need to step outside that comfort zone. Every single successful person, that ever lived, every single one of them has taken that leap of faith and stepped outside their circle of comfort, every single one, and there is a reason for that and that is because that is where things grow, or germinate at the very least. Humans are remarkable creatures, and we can create and do amazing things, but only if we believe we are capable of doing them. Now, I don't mean I believe I can fly, so I'm donna dive, head first, off this skyscraper. I mean, you would fly, for about a minute, then you would successfully and permanently fail. Remember, it's not the fall that kills you, it's the last three inches! Sit, optimistically, outside your comfort zone, but don't de a delusional dick about it. Don't think I can be an astronaut, then do nothing in your life to work towards that goal, unless you're Bruce Willis in Armageddon, then yeah, you can totally do nothing and still become an astronaut, but if you're not Bruce Willis, then you're fucked. No way you're going to be an astronaut! But, if you think I'm going to catering school, then I'm going to open my own restaurant, then a chain of them and become rich and successful and you

actually went to catering school, I'd be more inclined to believe you and your process.

Either way, it all comes down to the same old shit, you have to operate outside of your comfort zone. Learn to master that and the world is your lobster!

Yeah, yeah, yeah! It's all right for you O'Toole, you've already crushed your comfort zone and smashing goals. Well, I might have smashed one, but I'm no less susceptible to soul crushing doubt, I just know how to make it work for me now.

Make daily changes. The changes don't have to be big changes, just consistent. This kind of hot wires the thought process that change is possible.

If you can, find yourself a mentor. Mentors are the business! They rock. I've had a couple of mentors in my time and their sage advice is invaluable, especially if you find a great one. They do exist, they are out there and they will help. Actively seek one out, or keep your ears and eyes open for someone to help.

Try and learn something new. Putting yourself out there academically can be scary, but man, I adore learning. I usually have several courses on the go at the same time, and I probably always will. It doesn't matter what it or they are, just do something, but do something unexpected, out of the ordinary. I try and do something that makes people go "Gary? Gary's learning that! No way is he doing that!" Like hiphop dancing, I'm fucking fifty-five years old, my dumb white ass should definitely not be trying to do any hopping of my hip. I should be sat down with a great book and an even better cup of tea! But here we are, with me all ready to bust a sic move and feel the phat beat! I don't know if that made me sound cool, but I'm pretty confident it did. If not cool, definitely a little bit cool….er.

Face your fears. Face 'em people! Scared of singing, go take singing lessons. Scared of heights, go climb a mountain, just pick one with classes and do it under supervision and tutelage. That's what I did, and eventually had to repel, face forward, down a God damned mountain! I did that, me and you know what, it was absolutely brilliant. I totally enjoyed every single second of the entire day.

Remember to alternate or change up your challenges from physical to mental and back again, it's way much more fun that doing the same thing over and over again.

Up your game. We all know when we ain't bringing our **A** game, we all do it and we all know it and, if we are being honest, most of us don't do any more than just go through the motions with a task and no one ever bugs us about it, because everyone else is playing the same game. You know who's not playing it safe? Winners! They are pedal to the metal, flat our going for it. They are Usain Bolting it past our stagnant and lazy asses and on to victory, while the rest of us are left to wonder what the fuck just happened.

Perform a random act of kindness. I LOVE this one and I've done a couple of things. Firstly, I'll give a homeless person a cup of coffee and a chocolate bar whenever I can. I've spoken about this in a previous chapter and I have no intention to go on about it here.

Secondly, I go to the supermarket and spend around $10 getting some ransom household shopping-paper towels, a thin of baked beans, some teabags, biscuits and ketchup, stuff like that. Then I print off a A4 piece of paper that says:

You are the Recipient of a
R.A.O.K
Random Act Of Kindness.
Have a wonderful day x

Now take that shopping and that note and go to a suburb that's not very affluent and find a dilapidated, run down and unloved property, preferably one owned by a person that looks like they don't have a pot to piss in, or a window to throw it out off. Get out of your car, pick up the shopping and take it to that house. Without seeing the owner of the property, drop the shopping off and walk away. Don't wait to see who picks it up, or anything like that, just do your good deed and walk on. I guarantee, walking up to that front door will get you out of your comfort zone alright.

Take one single step. They say, who ever the hell they are, that the journey of a thousand miles starts with but a single step. Problem is, most people go-a thousand miles! Fuck that! And they never start the journey, it's just too daunting, but you know what's not daunting? A single step. A marathon, getting a PhD, writing a book, they all started with a single step towards our goals and little by little, we nudge ourselves along, until we can see the finish line and then, we finish! I'm no different to you, I'm just a normal bloke, but what I did was I broke my thousand miles into chapters, then paragraphs, then sentences and then words.

Truth is, in many ways, it doesn't matter what you chose to do, more that you have chosen to do it, whatever that it might be. You are pushing yourself out of your comfort zone and that will force you to grow.

WANNA GO PLAY?

Make new friends and influence people.

As I get older, you know what I learned? It's fucking lonely! And I blame Steve fucking Jobs and Mark fucking Zuckerberg! That's right, I went there and I'll even tell you why! Smart phones made people dumber and social media sites made people less sociable. I don't want to get into the whole 'In my day' bull shit, because, seriously, my day wasn't that long ago, BUT, in my day, you sat on a bus or in a cafe or, whatever, you went in and you talked to people. I bet, even if you are in your own home, let alone out and about, if you looked up, someone will be glued to their fucking phone liking a fucking TikTok! We are NEVER putting that gene back in it's bottle, that ship has well and truly sailed my friend, and one of the many downsides of this current trend is that people, in general, are far less adept at talking to other people and are, again in general, less likely to engage in the first place, and I get it, why talk to a stranger when you could be safe in your own bubble, protected from the chaotic noise of the world? But here's the thing, as with all skills, and communication is definitely a skill, the less you do it, the worse you get and no, it's not like riding a bike. The less you do, the less you want to do. Why do you think so many people consider themselves lonelier than ever, even when they are surrounded by people.

The thing is, that muscle memory stays with you, until eventually, you're old, cranky and if anyone tries to say hi, you internally say fuck it and fuck them! Now, I can't say with like any science behind it, that you will live longer if you surround yourself with family and friends you love and who love you, but I can say I believe it will make for a richer, fuller, more content existence, I mean seriously, how could it not? When we are kids, we make friends like it's easier than taking a piss in the deep end of the pool. You walk up to another kid in the park and say "Hey, you wanna play?" And they say yes or no, depending on their mood, or how bad you smell, but mostly I'd say it's 85% fuck yeah I wanna play, that'd be awesome and 15% Nah, stupid parent says I gotta go now, bye. As adults, we do this;

"Hey…."
"Fuck off weirdo, I don't fucking know you!"
"Yeah, I know, I was just wondering if you'd like to be fr…"
"I swear to God, I'll fucking stab you"

We have been seasoned and hardened (snigger) by time and experiences and we are just so much more resilient to the prospect of making friends. Also, we think disagreeing with something now-a-days is such a bad thing. Someone disagrees with you and instant burn! When I was a kid, I disagreed with my friends all the freakin' time.

"The Bionic Woman is hot, man"
"No way, Wonder Woman is way hotter"
"I think The Bionic Man is way cuter"
"Shut up Paul, always going on about The Bionic Man!"
"What?"
"We know you think he's hot"
"He is"
"Stop going on about your little Bionic Boner Paul"

And so it would continue.
Yes, we should have known better, but we were ten, give me a break.

We didn't like our friend any less because he loved Steve Austin, we all loved Steve Austin, he was the frickin' Bionic Man. We may not have loved him as much as Paul did and it was healthy and fun to disagree, but we always got over it, we always forgave and we always laughed about it. The older we get, the less we are prepared to let go and the less we are prepared to embrace. Best way around it, join something. I don't care what it is, a gym, a man's shed, a cookery class, amateur dramatics. Something that plonks you, slap bang, in the middle of someone else's comfort zone and way outside of your own. Here's one for the fridge door: In order for participation, there has to be perspiration. The simple fact is that loneliness and social isolation can, and often does, have an adverse effect on our mental and physical well-being, especially during these crazy Covid times (If you are reading this 100 years from now-yeah for me, my books still in circulation, but also Google Covid, you'll figure it out).

Friends will help prevent you from being isolated, good friends will stop you from feeling lonely. So, if you're isolated and lonely, what's gonna come next? Stress! Stress and anxiety, after all, who wouldn't get stressed and anxious at the thought of being isolated and lonely? I know I would. Studies have shown that increased stress can also lead to a poor immune health, insomnia, digestive problems, diabetes and high blood pressure. So now you're going to feel like shit and have no one to tell about it, how fucking awesome is that!

I have, on two seperate occasions, received and accepted hugs from complete strangers, exactly when I needed them, and how did they know that?

That was exactly what I needed and

That I would not only accept them, but be incredibly grateful for them? The answer is a little new age, but I genuinely believe they could sense it. They knew I needed a hug and the Universe gave those moments to me and I'm incredibly grateful for those very special moments. Occasionally we lose track of relationships and relations. I barely talk to my birth family, we never fell out, but our family unit was fractured when I was incredibly young and we never recovered, not even a little bit, it got worse after my father died and it got no better after the death of my mother (Who I really was not close to). I left home at fifteen, then spent the next eight years moving around all over the place, including almost three years backpacking around the world, which I loved. The up-shot was, unfortunately, that once I did decide to 'settle down,' I had no 'relationships' left. I'm still in contact with a couple of people from school and another couple from college, but for the most part, they have no more idea where I am, than I do of them. I am, essentially, alone, that's why, for me anyway, my family come first and always will. Now this isn't a woe is me chapter. I don't want you reading this thinking, damn he's fucked! I have several friends, my friend list is short, but significant, and I am content. I bring this up because I am a bright, loud, out-going optimistic person and I still have trouble. If you are a quiet, introverted, pessimistic person, you'd be forgiven for thinking there was no hope for you at all, but that's simply not true. You only need a chink of light to illuminate the darkest of rooms and sometimes, you just need that one person in your life to elevate you and brighten your day, even at its darkest.

When we are loved, when we feel as though we would be missed, we have a sense of belonging and we have a greater sense of purpose. There is a very famous chart called Maslow's Hierarchy of needs that states belonging is slap-bang in the middle of that chart, right below self-actualisation and esteem and above safety and The basics-think food, water and shelter.
So before food, water, shelter, security and stability comes a sense of belonging and love, and we all know this deep down. You could live in a mansion and be filthy rich, but if you are not loved,
you can be as miserable as sin, or you can be piss poor, but loved and feel like the cat that got the cream.

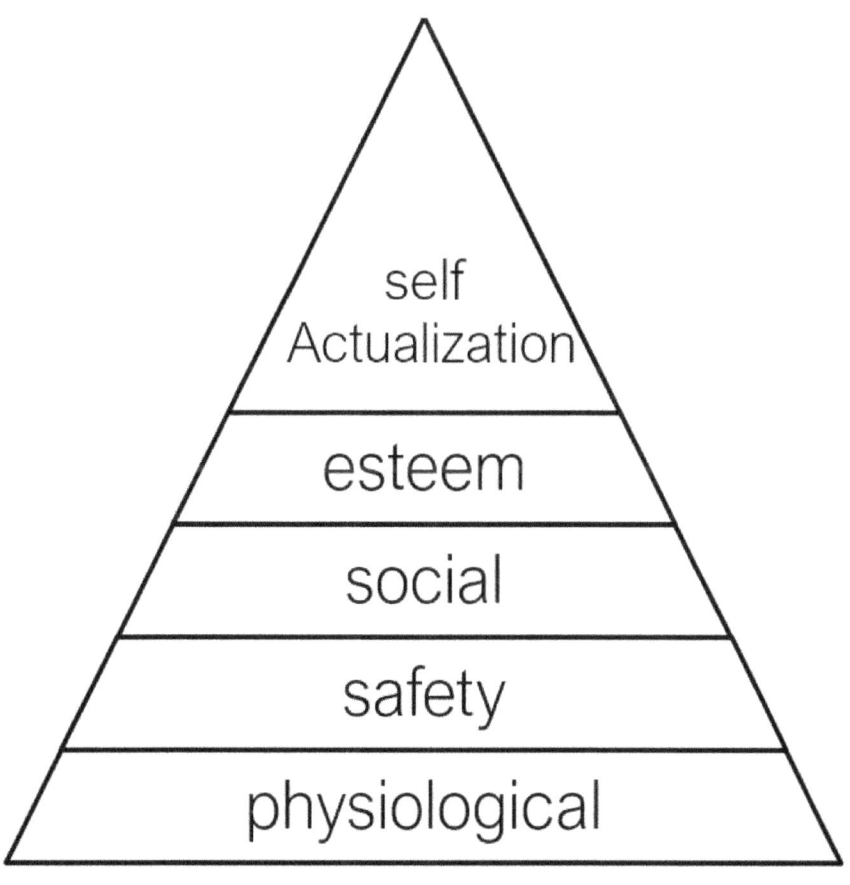

"One is the loneliest number that you'll ever do
Two can be as bad as one
It's the loneliest number since the number one'
Harry Nilsson 1968

Life, let's face it, can sometimes be pretty shitty and shit things happen all the time, even to nice people. Pan-fucking-demics! Divorce, deaths, unemployment… teenagers! Simple fact is, if you have a support network of friends to support you through these difficult times, it significantly alters how you initially deal with an issue and how you process it and process it, moving forward. Support just makes you stronger.

How do you build, grow, support and nourish these relationships? Well, first thing is PMA. What does PMA stand for though Gary? It sounds very new age. It's not. It stands for Positive Mental Attitude and this will help you push forward every single time. Successful people who think they are successful, are successful because they think they are successful! Mind officially blown!

Be the first to say yes! Make the first move for something. It doesn't have to be skydiving, it can be something super low key, like a book reading(?) Warm house, pot of tea, cheap packet of biscuits and away you go. Ask your neighbours, someone down the RSL, from work, a random stranger carrying too. Much shopping, do you need any help, do you need help stacking away the chairs after a meeting? Conversely, if you're asked to go to something like this, say yes. Look out for notices on your local community centre notice board, search the small ads in the local papers. There will be someone, somewhere, holding something, just say yes, or like I said, invite a small selection of people around to your place for a similar thing.

Stay in touch, or reconnect with people. Dig out the old telephone and address books, look on social media platforms, ask the friends you do have, do everything you can to make some form of connection. You could even try contacting your old school. They won't give out other peoples information, I'm sure, but you could say hey, here is MY contact details, please feel free to pass them on to anyone who was in my year at school. You could even place a free ad in the free paper in your local area. If you can't find a single soul, then find new ones, RSL, community centres, social clubs at work, hobby centred communities-magic, hiking, a favourite TV show, fuck it, if you can't even find one of them-create one yourself. Yes, some of this requires a degree of effort. To be honest, all of it requires a degree of effort, but putting on your shoes in the morning requires effort, just suck it up, take a deep breath and push forward, you'll be so happy you did.

Equally, sometimes we stick with people because the ones we have, are the only ones we've got. These people can create an artificially toxic environment, become toxic friends and end up causing you more stress than relief! Does your 'friend' always gossip about other people? Because I can virtually guarantee that while they are bagging out other people to you, they are bagging you out to other people. Is the relationship take, take, take? For example, I have a 'friend' who, if the conversation isn't about him, or what he's doing, then clearly it isn't a conversation with having (Roll eyes emoji). Does your friend make you feel pressured or manipulated into doing or saying something you don't want to? These are called Alpha Tops and we'll discuss them in a different book, but seriously, do they always make you feel pressured? Then what's the point of them? Do you feel like they always treat you like shit and never take your feelings into consideration? Do you always go to the movies when they want to go, see the film they want to see, share the cinema snacks they always chose? If you've got one of these, you only have two options; Tell them how they make you feel, tell them you don't like it and they have to stop treating you that way, you're going to have to stop being their friend, or shoot them in the head and bury them in the desert! NO! Sorry, WRONG answer, I meant to say drop them like a hot stone and never look back, they are not worth keeping, they really are not.

Good friends are good, great friends are priceless and as rare as hens teeth. One of the many things about a great relationship like this is that some things will remain the same, some things will change and grow, but year in and year out, your friends friendship, support and love will never falter. It will be a relationship built on trust and respect, honesty and yes, I said it already, love! Hold on tight to those relationships. They don't come around that ofter, and they incredibly precious and fragile and well worth protecting.

SO, THIS IS A YES DAY

Do something new.

Most people are dead the minute they are born and technically, that is true. We have a curtain number of minutes on this Earth and if, for example, you get to live till you are 85, that is 2,682,340,920 seconds or 44,705,682 minutes or 745,094.7 hours or 31,045 days… thirty-one thousand days, that's…… That is NOT a lot is it? Not really, not in the great big scheme of things. 31,000 days, plus change, and we start using them up from the very first second we are born, so if we are going to use them all up, let's use them up. Why not use them up wisely, or recklessly, depending on your particular point of view.

We are born, we are raised, we spend 10-15 yers in education, give or take, then we work for 50+ years, taking a holiday or two a year, if we are lucky. Then we retire and die a couple of years later from ill health or boredom! Fuck that! Who wants to live like that? Is that even living, or is it just existing until you're dead? You can break the chain, or if not break it, weaken it enough to hopefully enjoy your fucking life and one of the ways you can do that, is by doing something new. Now I'm not talking about a cultural revolution here, although some would say that was needed and on the cards.

I'm talking about a personal revolution, an individual revolution, a personal revolution, an existential revolution. If you can't follow your dreams, and why can't you follow your dreams? They are *your* dreams! Then do something new to facilitate them. Want the freedom to travel around the country for twelve months in a camper-van, whilst still earning an income and being stress free? Then take a copy-writing course and start earning some cash-I'd suggest you get established and working for six months+ before hand, or write a Vlog, or run an on-line business, or any number of different things to pay for petrol, food and utilities. Got kids? Take them with you. They pretty much home schooled all through 2020-2021 anyway, what's the difference now? We are talking alchemy here, mixing things up, change their order, their make-up, you turn their planned and ordered pre-destination onto its own head and see what is created. Life should be like that. The whole of life should be like that, how thrilling would that be? How alive would you feel then? Yes, of course, you have to plan for 'the future,' but you don't have to live your entire life by those rules, not quite yet. If, as a kid, you lived near a jetty or a pier, I bet in the summer, you'd run down that pier and jump off the end, into the inviting, crystal clear peppermint blue sea and splash and play until you could do it again and again and again, until you were exhausted, spent, used up and finished. If you went down that pier today, how many grown ups would you see jumping in? How many? The pier is the same, the sun is the same, the sea is the same. What changed? You, you changed and not for the better.

"Jumping in is just for the kids"

Fuck you! No, it's not and you know it's not and you know it's bull shit to say it is, so stop it. Stop using time or your bunions or whatever as an excuse, run to the end of that pier and jump off. Remember what it's like to feel to be alive! To be a kid. To run down the pier and jump off and feel alive.

I'm not 100% sure I have to do this, but just in case I do, can I please advise any and all readers of this book that, if you can't run or fucking swim, please don't jump off the end of the pier! (I can't believe I have to do that!)

Anyway, right back to it. Just do it, just jump. Have fun, take a risk or two, without breaking the law, and have some fun. It doesn't even have to be something that drastic. I've already mentioned all the things I currently have on my to do list from ukulele playing, singing, dancing, painting and Indian cooking, plus many more. Every day there should be something new. Something that challenges you, makes you think, makes you question, makes your horizons a little broader and harder to reach. Something to make you grow and blossom. Something that brings happiness and joy into your world and I don't know how to break this to you, but if you're waiting for someone else to do that for you, you'll be waiting a very long time. Most people are just trying to do for themselves.

It doesn't matter what it is. What matters is that you are taking the old, repetitive, mundane world and turning it on its head. You're not being defined or constricted by the boundaries of the 'old' ways. You are daring to take a chance, daring to take that proverbial leap of faith and if it doesn't work, what's the worst thing that could possibly happen, you get to learn German or The Ukulele? I've taken up knitting and lock picking-not peoples front doors you understand, this is just a clear plastic lock I can see the inner workings of, but as a massive and life long fan of everything Sherlock Holmes, the prospect of being able to pick a lock appeals to me. I think it's a pretty cool parlour trick to have up your sleeve.

If you fear something, you give it power, the more power it has, the more fear it generates. I'm not saying, if you have a fear of robbing a bank, you should rob a bank, that's dumb, but the principal applies. If you're scared of heights, sign up for a parachute jump. Better still sign up for a charity parachute jump and raise some money for a Noble cause, whilst simultaneously erasing one of your fears from existence, how cool would that be. You have to push and challenge and run towards the end of that pier every single chance you get, otherwise one day, you'll be in a nursing home, dribbling into your jello and pissing into a nappy, oblivious to the life you could have had. I'm going to paraphrase here, but a British adventurer called Bear Grylls once said we should get to heaven battered, bruised, covered in scars and completely used up and I couldn't agree with him more.

2,682,340,920
2,682,340,919
2,682,340,918
2,682,340,917
Time is forever ticking….

I'M OBJECTIONABLE

Disagree and question.

Before Karen came on the scene, people disagreed all the time. We were allowed to. We were encouraged to, it sparked discussion, debate and resolution. Now people are so twisted up in fear of saying the wrong thing, no one says a word. Petrified at the prospect of upsetting Karen, the Kraken of the moral code… only she's not! She's not the Kraken of the moral code. She's the Kraken of A moral code, hers, the one she wrote for herself, and she might think that book should be followed from immaculate dust cover to immaculate dust cover, but we don't have to follow Karen's moral code, fuck Karen and the code she rode in on. I don't give Karen one ounce of authority over my moral standing. I know what's right and wrong and I know what is morally, legally, socially and societally acceptable, we all do. We can question humour or jokes for example, you might not laugh. You might even find the joke offensive, but does that mean the joke shouldn't be said? It absolutely does not. Karen is offended, so what? I'm offended by her offence, now who's right? I'm not saying we should have *carte blanche* to be mean or rude, but offensive? NO, at worse, a 'bad' joke is subjective. You might find it rude and unfunny, I might find it hilarious and sharply observed.

You can find humour offensive, for sure, objectionable even, but should we still avoid telling the joke?

Most humour comes from a dark, hurtful place, the logic being, you can't truly enjoy the light without experiencing the darkness, but even I would agree, somethings should be a little more measured.

I don't have a problem, for example, of a joke about someone with Cerebral Palsy if it's being told by a person with Cerebral Palsy, but then what? Can white people only tell white jokes, Can gay people only tell gay jokes, or short people, or The Irish, should we be the only ones allowed to tell Irish jokes and yes, I'm counting myself as part Irish for this one, otherwise I'll never be able to tell another Irish joke, and I couldn't stand that. See?

Where does it start, where does it stop? Humour is universal. We should *all* be able to tell *all* jokes about everything, and if anyone tries to stop you, then they are oppressive and you should not tolerate that level of tyranny from anyone.

Disagree, debate, even agree to disagree, but don't be told what to say. You don't like what's being said, and you are in a position to do so, either argue your point, or leave, or wait for the other person to leave. If enough people agree with you, the other person will get 'it' pretty quickly, just as you'll get it if everyone else agrees with 'them'. Having said that, I don't want you loosing your job over a poorly judged joke and if you work in a company with a particularly crash hot HR department, then you might want to watch your step and your audience, but seriously, if Karen is offended by your jokes, don't tell your jokes in front of Karen. If Karen doesn't like it, Karen can fuck off. Now what we've spoken about up to now is a sense of humour, or lack there of, but the world is a great big onion and as a race of people, we can pretty much argue about absolutely everything. That's not a swig, it's a stick. That's not a stone, that's a rock, that's not a knife, this is a knife! Hang on, I slipped into movie quotes there! Point is, opinions are like arse holes, everyone's got one and they all stink! Sometimes we argue because it's fun (It's not fun, stop being a dick!) And sometimes, we seriously have to get our point across and sometimes those points elicit change and if that happens, it's fucking magical.

Politics, religion, never work with animals or children, stinky cheese, Irish whiskey or Scottish Whisky (It's Irish Whiskey every time. That was a trick question, because it wasn't really a question, because I already knew the answer and the answer is A Irish Whiskey). If you don't question, you don't grow, if you don't grow, you stagnate and if you stagnate, you will wither and you will die. We have to disagree and question, there's a very good reason a small child's favourite word is "Why?".

But, and there is always a but…. Do it with grace and diplomacy and respect. As far as the other person is concerned, *you* are wrong. *You* are the one being a dick and *you* are the one that has to be shown the right way of thinking about something. You, you, you. Whilst conversely, you're thinking them, them, them. Look at it this way, how many sides does a coin have? Two right, heads and tails. WRONG! There are three sides, heads, tails and the edge. You see, even when you KNOW, absolutely 100% that you are categorically right and nothing could possibly change your mind, there's always the edge, a thin slice of wriggle room. It's not big, there's not much to it, but it's powerful. It's what holds heads and tail together and it's usually where compromise is found.

We like people agreeing with us, it validates what we are saying and, let's strip away the bull shit for a moment, it makes us feel good, worthy even and it's way easier than confrontation.

It's just that I can't stand to see someone nudged out or belittled, it drives me crazy, so desire the fact that I don't actually like it, I like injustice less, so I swallow my bile and my pride and I speak up, but here's the thing, disagreements are inevitable. They are normal, they are supposed to happen, they usually happen for a reason and it's healthy that we have them. If we have all this disagreement pent up inside us and we never let it out, we either become the mad, old cat lady or the serial killer. I want to be neither. I work with 95% women, mostly nurses and surgeons and there is no way, on God's green Earth that I was ever going to be working in a conflict free environment. Everyone I work with is ramped up on hormones! Premenstrual, Menstruating, post menstrual premenopausal or menopausal. I'm like a lamb in a lions den every single time I go to work, I'm going to get letters for that one too! I will instantly retract it, of course, it's only a joke. My wife has just said "Do you know what's not a joke? MANsturation, your Meriod? Why are you so grumpy, are you having your MANopause?" I guess what goes around, comes around. I deserved that zinger! But, all the jokes aside, if conflicts are managed well, they can mostly have a positive outcome, hopefully, but even if a positive outcome isn't assured and you feel strongly enough about something to speak out, I don't think any decent person couldn't.

It also has to be said that, once you understand your 'opponents' point of view, and they see yours, it can lead to a stronger, fuller relationship and understanding. Or you can just quietly hate their guts and internally seethe about them at work and then externally rage about them at home. That's what home is for, right?

I'M NOT WRONG, YOU'RE WRONG, SHUT UP!

Admit when you are wrong, learn from it and don't do it again.

To be fare, I'm going to have to wing it on this one. Never having actually been wrong before, I'm just gonna have to Google the shit out of this subject and hope no one catches me out. I'll also have to consult with my family, especially my wife and my fifteen year old daughter, as they have a far greater understanding of what it's like to be wrong and fill in the blanks….

What a crock of horse shite! Of course I've been wrong. I've been wrong *so many times*, there should be a plaque up about me somewhere.

Here is the site where Gary O'Toole was wrong on at least one occasion. We believe there may be many, many more cases, but he was quite good at bull shitting.

I have been wrong a lot. Trouble is, I double down, I add a liberal dollop of bull shit to my denial and say it with such commitment that people begin to doubt themselves.

"Are you sure Sister Maria secretly worked for the Nazis in the Sound of Music?"

"You say Frank Sinatra was only four foot seven, and that's why he always wore hats, is that really a thing?"

"What do you mean, scientists discovered years ago that The Turin Shroud was actually a coffee stained tea towel?"

These are, obviously, no incidents of me being wrong, merely incidents of me bull shitting some poor simpleton into believing my bull shittiness. Like I said, I have wracked my brain, virtually tortured myself, trying to think of an incident where I've actually and genuinely been wrong and, I have to tell you, I'm pretty stumped.

I joke!

- When I was five, I tried to pick up a glass tumbler with my teeth, no hands-I still have the scar.
- I was convinced I could make the jump across the road with the ramp we built, to impress all the girls (2) that were watching. I got a massive black eye for that one, and a scar on my left knee.

- I was convinced I could do the 'knife trick' Bishop performed in Aliens. I couldn't. I still have the scar for that too.
- I've broke my nose more times than I care to remember, had my front teeth knocked out, been head butted and punched way too many times and I was once in a bar fight where someone got the tip of their nose bit off! I'd like to clarify that 1. I didn't bite the nose off 2. It wasn't my nose!
- I broke three bones in my right hand when I did push something I shouldn't have 1-0 telegraph pole.

And those are just some of the physical times I've been wrong. I've been intellectually, spiritually and emotionally wrong too and I'm going to blame my father's hot Irish blood for that, even though he was the most laid-back and chilled person I've ever met.

The thing about being wrong is, it makes you feel like a proper dick. It's humiliating, humbling and embarrassing. You want the entire world to swallow you up and spit you out a week later, but it never does. You just end up stood there, all sheepish, like you've just been caught with your dick in your hand, saying sorry and hoping you never have to go through the same thing twice, and that's the point, isn't it? If we don't actually learn from our mistakes, we are doomed to repeat them. The thing about mistakes is, we are allowed to make them, that's how we learn, but this isn't about mistakes. This is about being wrong and owning that, being accountable for that. We have ALL made mistakes, none of us are infallible, but when we are wrong, well, we just have to put our big boy pants on and say, you know what, I fucked up. I expected this to happen, this didn't happen, that happened and it all went to shit and it's my fault and I'm sorry and I'll do my absolute best to make sure it doesn't happen again. How simpler would life be if we could all do that? And I don't just mean in your house, or at work, or in the supermarket car park after a prang, but globally! If we, as a collective society, could learn to just do that one thing, I think that would be pretty awesome.

Being wrong and admitting to it are two seperate things of course, and who you are admitting your mistake to also plays into the situation. I'd be more inclined to admit I robbed a bank to a police officer than admit I ruined my wife's favourite blouse in the wash, or would I? Shouldn't it be the same, honest is honest, full stop. Shouldn't the over arcing principle remain the same, irrespective of what the 'crime' is, or who it happened to? That smells suspiciously like integrity to me, and the thing about integrity is, you can fake it for a while, but eventually you will be found out and that house of cards you built up around you to protect you, will come crashing down around your shoulders and snap your neck like a dried twig. What is the none gender specific equivalent of 'Man Up?' Person up? Let's go with that. Sometimes, you just have to person up and take your medicine, but that's only half the story, the other half isn't as complicated; LEARN what you did wrong, why you did it and how you did it and don't do it again, simple as that.

Equally, if you are the person being confessed to, it's important you learn how to appropriately respond to such a high degree of honesty. It took the person stood in front of you some guts to stand there, saying they are wrong. If your response is

"I knew it! I fuckin' knew it was you. Didn't I say it was you. Boy, Imma gonna make you pay for years for that fucking mistake! Every time you do something wrong, or even think about doing something wrong, I'm gonna remind you of this mother fucking moment and make you suffer like your life depends on it"!

If I'm going to get that response when I apologise, then sorry love, you're on your own. I'm having nothing to do with you or that conversation. You can think it wasn't me until I am on my death bed, and even then I'm not overly convinced you'll get a sorry out of me.

NB. I just checked with my wife and she confirms 100% that I've never been wrong or needed to say sorry for anything, so that's a bit of a win. If she changes her mind, I'll be sure to mention it in the next book.

AIN'T NO KID GONNA SAY YES TO THIS BS

Switch off the TV and other electronics.

Buckle in and prepare for a mind fuck, the likes of which you have yet to experience.

ACT Health recommended screen time limits.

For children aged 2-5 years of age*, sitting and watching television, and using other electronic media (DVDs, computer and other electronic games) should be no more than one hour per day. For children/young people aged 5-17 years**, limit sedentary recreational screen time to no more than 2 hours per day.

Australian Government, Department of Health (2017) Australian 24 Hour Movement Guidelines for the Early Years (Birth to 5 years)

**Australian Government, Department of Health (2019) Australian 24-Hour Movement Guidelines for Children & Young People (5-17 years)*

So, for years we have known how bad too much screen time is for our kids and for years we've said… fuck it! It's an easy baby sitter, it's not worth the fights trying to take it off them, I'm happy for them to be on their devices, it gives me some 'me' time. We have become the holy trinity of child caring parents, lazy, ignorant and indifferent. Yes, I did just say that, we have become lazy, ignorant and indifferent parents. In fact I'd go so far as to say we have allowed our children's devices to become surrogate parents. We are failing our children in the most spectacular and appalling fashion and there doesn't seem to be an end in site, and why? Because our electronic devices have become surrogate children. We sit and stare and swipe and like just as much as our children do. They have learned to live without us, and we have learned to live without them, and I think that is the saddest indictment on human nature I have ever had the misfortune of having to write.

I don't blame the kids, they know no difference. The iPhone has been available since 2007, so if you've got a fifteen year old kid, they have never lived in a world without iPhones. Double tapping a 'like' is as natural to them as reading a book is to us. This is not the children's fault, as parents, it is ours and I get it, trying to remove an electronic device from a Childs grasp is fucking difficult, sometimes impossible, except it is NOT impossible, it's just easier to say it's impossible. That way we don't have to deal with the fallout once we've taken it off them. The attitude, the door slamming, the arguments, the sullenness, all that wonderful crap, as parents, we have to deal with. The thing is, like I mentioned, it's not all the children's fault. One child psychologist I spoke with said taking a child's device off them is worse than chopping off their arm, literally. The anxiety, the fear of missing out, the peer pressure, all of that can be overwhelming for a child and the thing is, sure, as part time parents, we helped get them there, but as much as it's not all their fault, and it's not all our fault either. It's everyone's fault and no ones fault, all at the same time, and we are a long way past proportioning blame, now we just have to deal with it.

Now, in the interest of full disclosure, I'm the last person to be able to tell anyone how to raise their kids. Mine are pretty good kids, but they are not role models, any more than I am. Besides, I have just as much trouble prying their iPhones out of their hands as the next parent, but the ACT are here to help yet again, with some helpful hints for reducing screen time.

Ways you can limit screen time

It could be challenging limiting the kids 'screen time but these tips may help.

- Set family rules about the maximum time on screens per day and stick to it
- Try not to leave the TV on in the background – use music instead

- Designate certain days as screen-free days (this could be one or two days during the week when they have other after school activities)
- Encourage children to be selective about what they watch rather than just whatever happens to be on
- Have a "no screen" policy during meal times
- Avoid having screens in bedrooms or study/quiet areas
- You could use a timer or alarm clock to enforce the screen time you set
- Try not to spend lots of time in front of a screen, or let the kids see you spending lots of time in front of a screen
- Wherever possible, choose non-screen-based activities and entertainment.

So there you go, simple as that really (eye roll emoji) Truth is, this is all very good advice, great advice even, but it only works because of one thing-you! You are the bedrock on which these rules will fail or thrive. You will lead the way. You will set the pace. Your kids won't, your kids will sabotage your efforts at every single turn. They will make you doubt yourself, question your sanity and tie you into mental knots, in the hope you'll just raise your hands to the heavens and scream, through clenched and chipped teeth, fuck it! I can't deal with this shit any more. But be strong, be persistent and be consistent and you will prevail.

Despite everything they say, and everything they do to convince you otherwise, kids need structure and form to move forward through life as well rounded, functioning members of society. Apart from Ralph, who still plays on-line gaming till four in the morning, in his mums basement/Ralph-Cave, whatever he's calling it between power-ups and dry wanking into his used, ironically names, sports socks! Fuck you Ralph, fuck you, and grow up and get a job and move out of your moms basement, you lame bastard! (I felt that needed to be said for all the Ralph mums out there)

I kept this chapter specifically short, not because I didn't have lots to say. There's mountains of information available about the benefits of limiting screen time, but I wanted to provide something that was short enough for your kids to read. Perhaps put a post-it or two over the Ralph comments, if you want to protect your little darlings. If your little darling is called Ralph and he refuses to grow up and/or move out, then let the little prick read it all and fuck you Ralph, fuck you!

WHAT IS MY WHY?

Set goals and evaluate often

Big ones, little ones, realistic ones, optimistic ones and rational ones and bonkers ones. We should all be setting goals, achieving goals, evaluations goals and setting new ones as the old ones get fulfilled, or fall from our list.

Goal

noun

noun: goal; plural noun: goals

The object of a person's ambition or effort; an aim or desired result.

"He achieved his goal of becoming King of England"

Alanis Morissette would swear it was all a little too ironic, all this setting goals BS, when chances are, you'll soon enough forget the damned things and all that work and effort will be for nothing. Well, that would be true I suppose, if you actually did forget all those whispered promises to yourself, but the real truth is, you never actually forget those promises, those goals. They are embedded deep in you, they are promises you made or make to yourself, for the life you wish to live and who the hell doesn't want to live their best life? Why would you even settle for second best, and yet, that's what billions of us do every single day. Our dreams are too big, to etherial, to whimsical, to short sighted, far fetched, not thought out, thought out too much. Bull shit, bull shit, BULLSHIT! Your dreams don't actuate for a number of reasons, least of which is that they are too grand in scope for the Universe to comprehend, fathom or materialise.

I was told by one of my mentors once to write down my goals. Actually, physically write them down on a piece of card, about the size of a credit card. I was required to write five goals, things I wanted to achieve and an end date for that to happen. I loved my mentor, he was hypnotic and I did what I was told, I wrote them down. Now I had to take that card out of my wallet every day and read it, read it whenever I had a spare minute. I had to read from beginning to end, my five essential goals. If I was upbeat about achieving a goal, read it. If I was feeling low, read it. If I had a win, or a loss, or no one gave a fuck or changed their minds, read it. If I achieved a goal, I would take a new card and move the goals up, simultaneously creating a 'new' number five goal. There is a very strange thing that happens to your brain when you physically manifest your goals, even in list form, on a small piece of card you pop in your wallet or purse. The actual act of externally creating the list, it provides you something to physically draw your attention to, they are no longer wishy-washy mind goals floating around in your big, stupid, melon. They become more 'real' because not only can you see them, but everyone you share them with can see them too and sharing a goal, that's scary shit right there, but even if the only person who reads them is you, what writing them down does is give you something to aim for.

What it also does is give you a greater understanding of what your goals are and what priority you give them. For example, you might think your number one goal is to become rich and famous, but when you write them down, you discover making money is number two and being famous is number seven. So which one to you focus on first? You focus on number one, stupid! And with that focus, what you get is a clearer picture of what you have to do, from this moment on, to achieve that goal. You now have a clearer focus, clarity in your decision making process, motivation and greater control of your future, and let me tell you, you have a focused future and a road map, you're already two hundred steps beyond most of the bozos out there.

Right, pay attention stupid, because this one is a game changer, a life changer and it's something you have to do… Whenever your plan doesn't go according to plan, and your plan will go to shit often, you will stumble and fall, and you WILL stumble and fall many, many times (As your plan turns shit). You stop your sorry ass from crying, you pick yourself up, dust yourself down and keep pushing forward. You stay down, you're never getting back up. Through every bad word said by your loved one, your family or your friends, bad reviews, Sucky interview, all the shit and humble pie you've had to shove down and gag on, every single time! None of that will matter in the end. None of that will matter when you step over that finish line.

HOW TO GET TO CARNEGIE HALL

Don't expect instant change. Practice doesn't make perfect, it makes progress and progress is what brings the perfection.

Well, holy fuck! We are here. We are at week fifty-two! Damn! So what do I mean exactly by "Don't expect instant change. Practice doesn't make perfect, it makes progress". Well, I like to think of it a bit like walking. I absolutely couldn't do it when I was born, I just lay there, like a demanding Witchetty grub, filling my nappy and demanding food. When I got to around eight months old, I started to 'dabble' with the notion of walking. I'd seen all the cool kids do it and I was I as like;

"Yeah, I can do that. I'm gonna crush it…"

Splat!

Splat!

Crash!

Boom!

Flat on my face, or my ass. Either way, walking was not for me. I mean, I put my heart and soul into that mother fucking walking, and I didn't get any return on my efforts at all! I mean, I couldn't even stand without looking like Uncle Barry, stood at the bar on a Saturday night. All red faced, scrunched up, watery eyes and wibbly wobbly bendy legs, but I never gave up. I tried and failed, tried and failed, tried and… fuck me, I'm standing! Then I took a step, then I took two. Eventually I could stagger across the room from one parent to the other without falling on my padded, ass. Flash forward a couple of months and I've got a mother screaming after me like a damned Banshee, wondering where the hell I was and why I wouldn't stop moving? I've not stopped moving since and praise the Lord for it. Now, I'm pretty sure most of us went through that struggle.

I'm also confident that 99.999% of us can't recall our first baby steps anywhere near as well as our parents do. Most studies estimate that we don't actually start forming memories until we are approximately two and a half, but I sure as hell remember the aftermath of that learning experience because I'm still walking!

I didn't 'try' walking once, fell over and through "Fuck it, Imma just gonna slide everywhere from now on" No, that's not what happened. It happens to virtually everyone on the planet and walking is a skill we acquire. It takes months and months of practice (and failure) before we can turn around and advise the world "I CAN WALK"

Practice made progress. From sat still, to crawling, to walking, to running my chubby little ass off. Without progression, we will not continue with anything new. If we are learning another language, for example, if after six months of trying, we couldn't even say hello or goodbye, we'd totally give up. Practice at anything, practice with determination, and you will succeed and that means focusing on the long term goals, as well as the short term ones. You can say to yourself, right, at the end of this month, I'm going to learn and remember the phrase "Good morning Madam, how are you doing" in German, but if you haven't practiced, it's not going to happen. It sounds stupid when you read it right? Like, of course I'm not going to learn German, if I've not actually studied German, but you'd be amazed at how many people feel entitled to just about everything. Point is, don't let your inexperience of anything stop you from doing it. Virtually everything we do, from walking, talking, cooking, cleaning, interacting, everything. Virtually everything we do, we have been taught. They are skills. We have some instinctual components kick in, fight or flight type of situations, but for the most part, we learn stuff. That's what makes us unique in the animal kingdom and why we became number one, so if you want to learn the Saxophone at seventy-six, you go buy a Saxophone. You have a partner who's first language isn't the same as yours and you want to impress the shit out of them, and also know what their relatives are saying about you, then learn their language. You can do whatever you want to do. You can achieve whatever you want to achieve, you just have to practice, practice, practice and, as I've mentioned in this book before, it takes around twelve weeks to form new neurological pathways, so stick with something for 12 weeks and after that, things will get better and easier. It becomes easier to practice 4pm to 5 pm Monday, Wednesday and Friday, because that's what you always do. Your brain and body clock will associate those times with learning and you'll just slip into it. What you are learning might not become any easier, but your ability to structure that learning definitely will.

You might not even be learning something. It might be that you want to do Yoga, exercise or catch up with friends. You might even want to sit down in Covid and write a book called How Not To Be A D**K, now wouldn't that be something!

Conclusion.

Congratulations, you are well on your way to not being a dick! You've picked up and read this book called How Not To Be A Dick, which means, in general terms, on some level, some deep rooted and untapped level, you recognised in yourself a degree of dickishness and that my friend, right there, that's a good thing, now you have begun to change and grow and be better people, good shit like that. Not being a dick is hard work. It's hard work, sometimes thankless work and constant work. There is no end destination here, your life journey is, in itself, it's own destination, but can you really stop trying to be a dick? Isn't that something a dick would do? Over time, it will take less and less effort. In time, it may take no time at all and if, on occasion, you revert and you are a dick again, don't beat yourself up. We all have the capacity to be a dick, once in a while, but we also have the capability and capacity to move away from who we were, to become who we believe we should be, but also, don't beat yourself up too much. If I think of the nicest person I can think of, who we can all relate to, I'd have to say Tom Hanks, the American actor. If I think of a genuine, nice, all round decent person who isn't a dick, I'm going to think Tom Hanks, but even when I think of Tom Hanks, I know, deep down, on some level, Tom Hanks has the capacity to be a complete dick, and if Tom Hanks can be a dick, what chance do you have?

I wish you nothing but success. May the blue bird of happiness continue to shit on you from a great height. May you learn the things you want to learn, embrace the things you want to embrace and accept the things you cannot change, to make a more confident, kind, stronger and more giving and vibrant version of who you already are.

I hope you've enjoyed this book as much as I have enjoyed writing it. It's been fun and insightful and informative, as much for me as anyone else. I am on this 'journey' too, of course, and have much left to learn. My only hope is that if we meet at a party, or a book signing or the supermarket, you don't go away thinking what a dick! The only time you're allowed to say that is if we are stood next to each other in a public urinal and you look down and take a peak, but even then, just think it, don't say it. You say it and it just gets real weird.

And they all lived happily ever after…

THE END

www.ingramcontent.com/pod-product-compliance
Lightning Source LLC
Chambersburg PA
CBHW070257010526
44107CB00056B/2488